TABLE OF CONTENTS

INTRODUCTION

This book is about the *business* side of planning, producing, and distributing effective motion picture films. Our interest is in films that not only satisfy a specific communication requirement for your client but also represent a profitable venture for you, the producer.

There has been extensive documentation in recent years on the *aesthetic* side of filmmaking, addressing the mechanical aspects—such as the cameras, films, lights, and filters, as well as the setting, casting, story, and so on. Little, however, has been written directly to the producer explaining how to run an ongoing, profitable business in the realm of nontheatrical filmmaking.

We think you will find that *The Business of Filmmaking* fills that gap rather effectively. Since any business activity requires clients, the book begins in Part One with the problems of finding potential clients, planning client sales calls, determining client communications needs, and reaching agreement on the need for a film. In Part Two, we cover writing a successful film proposal, preparing a preliminary film budget, and getting a signature on your production contract. Once you are in production, Part Three will guide you through production data collection and cost control. Part Four will help you during the postproduction phases of your film. Distribution and promotion of the finished film are discussed in Part Five. And Part Six wraps up all of those "other things" you ought to know about business—financial records, depreciation of equipment, balance sheets, symptoms and causes of business failure, and more.

Although the independent nontheatrical film producer is our primary audience, this book should also be of considerable interest to in-house producers in business and industry, government, education, medicine, and television. And clients of filmmakers will benefit from reading *The Business of Filmmaking* by being better prepared to interact knowledgeably with a producer on new film projects.

If this entire book could be

summarized in a phrase, we might say "take the next step." As a producer, well-developed photographic and aesthetic skills are essential to your success. The next step—that of gaining skill in the financial planning and administration of your business—should help you to be even more successful. Not at all coincidental, you will find quotes from a new Kodak informational film entitled *The Next Step* placed strategically throughout Part One of the book. Dr. Ted Levitt (Professor in Business Administration, Harvard Business School) and Mr. James C. "Denny" Crimmins (President, Playback Associates, New York City) appear in the film and candidly discuss how a producer can most effectively market his or her skills and services.

PART ONE—
MARKETING THE FILM CONCEPT

FILM AS A BUSINESS TOOL

Knowing how to make a film—knowing how to use the medium to communicate a message—is not enough if you are to become successful. You must also know how to *communicate* with people who need the films so that you can get a chance to use your creative talents. In business, that's known as marketing.

Your marketing should begin with a sensible look at what you have to offer. In reality, film is not what you have to offer. What you have to offer are solutions to problems, using film as the medium for communication. That's what nontheatrical filmmaking is all about.

There are several areas open to the nontheatrical filmmaker—business, education, special interest groups, vacation resorts, governmental agencies. All have a use for sponsored nontheatrical films—films that teach, films that promote, films that pass along information. But the single largest market existing today for nontheatrical films is business. You're going to find most of your work in business because every business has communication problems that *must* be solved in order to stay in business.

Basically, there are three types of communication problems in business: those related to skill and knowledge, motivational problems, and problems of information; and, of course, some business communication problems are a combination of the three.

Problems in the skill-knowledge area usually involve situations where an employee lacks the understanding necessary to perform a job. People have to be trained to make products. People have to be instructed in safety procedures. People have to be coached in selling the product. The idea is this: People who know more about their jobs are more effective. That's a good investment.

In the motivational area, the problem is that even though some employees can do a job, they may not *want* to do it. Most companies recognize that people who want to work are more productive and will work harder toward a solution to the problem. Motivational problems can also involve a company's prospective clients. The solution in this case can usually be found in the area of more effective advertising and sales promotion.

In the informational area, the problem is what most people would refer to as "public relations." Corporate and product visibility is very important to most companies, since exposure and goodwill help sell products. A company that perceives a need for solving informational problems will invest in the solution that best reaches its audience.

The point is, business spends money to make money. A smart businessperson will provide the money to make a film once there is an understanding that film will help solve a problem. Your job is to discover where a film will help.

"Trade journals will tell you what's going on and what kinds of films are being made and who's making them. Also, industries will address business problems in their annual reports .... Read the business page in your newspaper; look to see where trends are happening."

There may be several people to contact in each company. Internal structures are easy enough to penetrate if you keep the communication needs in mind. One way to get started is to call the switchboard or drop by the lobby, and ask questions:

"Could I speak to the manager of the Training Department?"

"Who is in charge of Sales Promotion?"

"I'd like to talk to someone in Corporate Relations."

. . . and so on. It may take a while, but most people are helpful once they understand that you are trying to find someone you can show your talents to.

Within each company there may be several different departments that have a need for film. You will find that department names vary greatly—AV Services, Advertising and Sales Promotion, Media Services, Marketing Development—but their purposes are all the same: to solve communication problems. Somewhere in these departments you will find one or more prospects. They may deal directly with you; on the other hand, they may be required to request the work through a central media department. Don't forget, a company with one prospect for you probably has two.

"Organizations (business corporations, universities, churches, hospitals) have internal communications problems, such as training their employees, communicating government regulations and rules, motivating people, and creating a sense of community among their people so they work as teams; those are common problems for any kind of organization."

FINDING POTENTIAL CLIENTS

Every company is a potential client. First, start with a list of companies in your area. Use the phone book, a Chamber of Commerce listing, the *Fortune 500,* trade listings. Some companies, because of size, will be obvious prospects. Of course, if those companies use film, they probably have many other filmmakers calling on them already. But you have nothing to lose by offering your services as well. It's true that you may not have anything to offer that they are not getting now, but you'll never know unless you contact them.

"To reach individuals in a company, you have to first work through the 'corporate tree' and pick the branch that you feel needs a film."

A second way to get potential clients is to offer them a solution to a problem you perceive before you ever meet. This involves a good deal of homework. Look in trade journals, annual reports, and business papers and magazines. Each will give you an idea of current business problems. It may spark an idea that you can develop into a proposal. Once your ideas are thought out, place a few phone calls to the company until you find someone who is willing to briefly discuss your idea. If that person seems interested, you can send the full proposal for further investigation.

If the company is not interested in that particular proposal, you will have shown yourself to be someone interested in solving its problems, and that alone may help you get some work.

And don't forget that your prospects may be working with cyclical budgets. For example, the textile industry will probably be most busy twice a year and will have to introduce new products—in the spring and fall. Car manufacturers come out with their new products in the spring and fall. Summer recreation has an obvious selling period, as does winter recreation. Budgets for producing work become available before those selling periods. So, your marketing efforts have to coincide with the budgets, not with the selling periods. Direct your efforts toward the future; if your prospect doesn't have money now, the money will come eventually.

"What you have to get a little more aware of, and perhaps a hell of a lot more aware of, is corporate budgeting. Corporate budgets have certain approval cycles, certain processes, and there are times that you can get at the money and times that you can't. You don't want to do all your homework and then go in there and find that there's no water in the well."

Before you ever reach a potential client's desk, you have to decide *why* you are going to meet with that person. Certainly you want to introduce yourself and, if possible, show some samples of your work. But you should be trying to do more than that so that you can best define what you have to offer. Among other things, you will want to find out what communications needs exist in the company, how these needs are currently solved, and whether the person you are talking to has the power or influence to hire you.

When you meet someone for the first time, you have the opportunity to begin a lasting business relationship. You must take control. You know what you can do. Now is your chance to find out what you can do for your prospect. You can only do that by determining what your prospect needs.

DETERMINING CLIENT COMMUNICATION REQUIREMENTS

There are two ways to approach a communication problem. One way is to let the client take control; you do that by talking about yourself, your attitudes, your previous successes with other similar problems. This approach is not particularly successful. A more effective way is to take control yourself—define your meeting; you're there to get business. You can help yourself by paying attention to the problem. Listen to what the client has to say and ask questions that will reveal why your client thinks of the problem as unique.

But it's not enough for you to discover your client's needs. You also have to help the client really understand the needs and reach agreement on them. Only when you have reached that point can you begin to talk about solutions. You may have to hold several meetings before you begin to talk about film, which is just the medium for solving the problem.

"You have to find out first of all how they think, how they operate, what their business is like, how they make decisions."

The importance of good communication skills in determining your client's needs cannot be overestimated. Remember, you are in marketing as well as filmmaking. Marketing requires certain skills that you may never have considered.

Keep in mind that your job is to solve your client's problem. You may understand the problem one way; your client may understand the problem differently. You must learn to listen carefully and question your client skillfully so that you can both agree on a definite solution to the problem. You may be able to create a great film; but if your client isn't happy, it may be your last film.

Believe it or not, you may not listen very well. Listening is a difficult thing to do well. It requires much concentration. Speaking takes more time than hearing, so our minds have time to wander. We've all been in situations where we pretended to listen, even appeared to be listening, when actually our thoughts were somewhere else. That can be a problem. How can you understand what your prospect wants or needs unless you understand what is said? You can't understand what is said unless you listen.

You will find, with practice, that there is a difference in the way you listen to people. Some people—marriage partners or close friends—you understand instinctively. Other people have difficulty expressing themselves clearly, and you have to concentrate to understand what is being said. Some make practice of masking their true feelings; with these people you often have to listen for what they mean and not what they say.

So, as long as your mind has some spare time, you can use it to "read between the lines." For example, if your prospect tells you a "dynamic" film is needed, you might take the time to wonder if that means a film with dynamic production values or a film about a dynamic company.

In the same vein, you have to learn to combine what you hear with what you see. Body language can be more

things that are important to your objective. But you can't let yourself become so anxious that you change what the prospect says into something you want to hear. If you do, you're liable to offer a ready-made solution to a problem that the prospect doesn't have, and you'll lose your credibility, at least. Be patient. Hear the prospect out. If you don't understand, ask for clarification—that's flattering to anyone. It shows you care. You have to have empathy if you want to really understand what the

expressive than words. It's the visual cues that give depth to an actor's performance, for example. We give each other the same kind of nonverbal messages in everyday life. Are your prospect's visual cues contradictory to what is being said? Does the prospect say one thing but mean another? Do the verbal and nonverbal communications make sense together? If not, then what is the prospect really saying? Do you find your prospect staring out the window or looking at the clock? If so, do you suppose you're not on the same wavelength? Maybe you're just talking too much.

Don't forget that listening is a form of persuasion. People like to be listened to and understood. It is complimentary. It means you are interested in them and their problems.

Good listening is learning. We tend to hear what we want to hear, not what is being said. It is important to keep an open mind about what another person says—or keep your bias out of the conversation. Sure, you want to pick out

prospect sees as needs. You will be doing yourself a favor if you leave your mind open enough to understand your prospect's frame of reference.

Another problem we can have with listening is in distinguishing between important points and unimportant points. It usually indicates that we don't know what we're specifically looking for. Clients and prospects have the same problem; many don't know what they're looking for. Many people try to do too much with one film—they want to appeal to greatly different audiences, or they want to cover too many points to convey significantly different messages. It is up to you to listen for the important points so that you can help them discover the most effective solution.

Finally, when you're listening, don't forget to look like you're listening. Sometimes we get so caught up in listening that we forget to let the other person know that we *are* listening. Good listening involves a certain amount of politeness—the social conventions like "uh-huh," "yes," nodding the head, keeping eye contact, appearing interested; all these things encourage a person to continue talking and consider you for the job.

Look at listening as having three levels. The first is the nonhearing level. That is, not listening at all. The second is simply hearing. Most of the time, when we just hear something, we can't remember what was said later on. The third level is the thinking level of listening. That is, evaluating what was said, analyzing it, comparing it to other statements, predicting outcomes, finding directions, and so on. A prospect who listens on the thinking level will visualize your ideas in action—in the way the prospect could either use them or find them useless. When you are trying to influence someone, you can't just talk about your ideas; you must stimulate your prospect to think about them—to try them on to see how they fit. You can stimulate a prospect to think by asking the right kinds of questions—questions that get the prospect to talk about your ideas, to try them on; questions that point to solutions; questions that lead the way.

The way you ask questions determines both the amount of information you get and the amount of stimulation you can provide to get the prospect to think about you and what you have to offer.

You need the answers to six basic questions: who, what, when, where, why, and how. There are two ways to ask those questions. To get background, you ask questions of a general nature:

"Would you tell me about your use of motion pictures?"

"How would you describe your training goals?"

"How are you planning to introduce your new products?"

"Why do you feel that way?"

When you want specific answers, ask specific questions:

"How many people will you be training?"

"Who reviews film proposals?"

"How many titles are there in your film library?"

The answers you receive will help fill in the details of the prospect's needs. They can also help you lead the discussion, clarify a point, or get agreement.

The key to asking questions is in knowing the kind of answer you're looking for or the kind of information you need. Both kinds of questions have a place in your conversations with prospects.

The general questions can give you much information, but they can also lead you away from your objective; the specific questions can give you answers you need, but too many at one time can seem like a cross-examination. You have to be sensitive to your prospect and pace yourself accordingly. Usually, you will want to start a new topic—a new thought—with a general question and then narrow the response with specific questions until you have all the information you need. But get to the point, stick to the point, and don't take more time than is absolutely necessary on any particular subject. The important thing is to get the prospect involved and interested, not just to practice making conversation.

Once you have asked your question, be silent. Give the prospect a chance to think about the question and to answer it fully. No one likes to be interrupted. If you ask a question and don't get an answer right away, don't ask another question—wait. Some people like to think over several answers before speaking. So, keep quiet. You'll get an answer sooner or later. And you can't act on the answer unless you listen to it. Dealing with pauses requires considerable self-discipline, but it's worth it. The time you wait gives the prospect a chance to mull over what you have been presenting. You need time to think when you buy something, and so do your prospects.

Taking control of the situation also means understanding how to respond to different types of people. Some prospects may start talking as soon as you come in, telling you everything there is to know about their organization. Great. Listen to what is said, because no matter how wordy the prospect may be, you are getting the information you need to decide whether you can help.

Some other prospects may not want to talk at all. They may want to know everything about you and the work you've done in the past. Maybe they just want to get to know you so that they can feel comfortable in talking with you. Fine. Tell them everything that is relevant. But at some point, you have to turn it back to them. Ask them if your experience might be useful to them.

Some people may tell you every reason in the world for not working with filmmakers. This is your best opportunity to get the information you need to keep marketing. Because every time your prospect objects, you can ask: "Why do you feel that way?"

Some prospects may tell you about their problems but not really want to take the next step with you. These people are a little less daring; a little less ready to take the next step. You have to give them something to decide on. You have to say . . .

"Could you tell me a little more about this project specifically?"

"What do you need to get this project off the ground?"

"I have some ideas about this project. I'd like to write up a proposal and meet with you again next week."

Good questioning and good listening are just techniques for getting inside a person's mind. Put yourself in your prospect's place. Get that person to participate. Don't forget, you are in control. And it's up to you to position yourself as a person who is able to present ideas and to respond to them intelligently.

"It seems like two analyses simultaneously. One is an analysis of what people out here need; another is an analysis of what I have to take to those people and hopefully find a common bridge or several common bridges."

Some people think of their prospects, or their clients, as narrow-minded individuals who get in the way of their creative work. Although there is a certain

amount of truth in that, as there is in any business, the great majority of people are just as ambitious as you are and desire just as much as you do to put out a good piece of work. The difference is that you know how it works. Remember, they have the problems, and you have the *solutions* to the problems. One of your jobs is to educate them on the possibilities you have to offer. However it turns out, your work must reflect their needs.

REACHING AGREEMENT ON THE NEED FOR A FILM

At the end of your first meeting with a prospect, some action has to be taken if you are going to continue to work with the prospect and perhaps do a film. This, again, is continuing your control. In business, this point in the action is called a *close.*

What it means is that you must get your prospect to agree to do something. You may have to suggest what to do next. It may be to write a proposal, meet with other people, or continue discussing how you might help the company. You have to do *something* or the prospect is lost to you.

If you continue to work with the prospect, you will find that at every point along the way there are places where action must definitely be taken. For example, when you have submitted a proposal, you have to take action on the proposal which in many cases is simply to ask: "Shall we go ahead with it then" or "Does it meet with your approval?"

When you ask for a positive action and the prospect says "No," don't give up, not yet. First, take the time to find out why your prospect has said no. It may be that the proposal you have submitted doesn't clearly solve the problem. In that case, your job is easy; just write another proposal. Perhaps the client isn't convinced that you can do the job. In that case, you can ask the client if

references from other people would be helpful.

Whatever you do, don't let the word "no" stop you until you find out why. And when you find out why, close—that is, take an action that will get you a "yes."

At some point in the filmmaking process—before you begin production—you will have to communicate with people who hold the purse strings . . . you will have to get the proposal approved. Even though your client may understand the creative and technical aspects of filmmaking as well as you do, somewhere along the line you will have to talk to people who relate to costs differently than you. Keep in mind that your client's company doesn't need a film *per se,* it needs solutions to problems. The film you create will have to solve those problems in cost-effective ways. It goes back to the three kinds of communication needs. Ask yourself a few questions: Will the company be able to sell more products? Will it be able to train people better? Will it now be able to communicate information to more people more effectively? Will the employees be sufficiently motivated by the film to justify the cost of producing it?

All of these questions are related in one way or another to profit. If the company can sell more goods and services, get more work done, disseminate more necessary information using audiovisuals, and if it can get more in return than it spends on your film, then that is a gain for the company and the kind of "bottom line" that interests those who have final approval of the project.

"What gives a company the results it's looking for? A film may be *your* end product, but it's not *their* end product . . . film is a medium you give them to help solve their internal or external communication problems."

To summarize, finding and keeping clients is a sequential marketing process. Even though you are only marketing yourself, there is a logical order of steps to go through in order to get down to the business of making a film.

Basically, it involves doing things one step at a time. First, you have to decide where the potential jobs are. Second, you have to find out whom to talk to. Before you ever see that person, you have to do some homework in two areas. Find out as much as you can about your prospect's organizational setup and communication needs. Then, decide what it is you have to talk about so you can present yourself properly.

When you see the prospect, you will go through a series of steps involving questioning and listening to find out the communication needs of the prospect and of the company. Once you know these needs, you have to present yourself as a person—a filmmaker—who can offer some solutions. And, if the prospect looks good, you have to close—which means that, if nothing else, you decide when to meet again to talk more specifically about certain projects or needs within the company.

After you have a project or perhaps an order to get a project, you have to write a proposal based on the objectives that you and your client have worked out. You may even have to write a second proposal detailing the business advantages to the company as well as alternative proposals.

And finally, you have to secure a contract before you begin production. At this point, your marketing job is not over. Even though you are now concentrating most of your efforts on making the film, you must still stay in close contact with your clients to keep them up-to-date on the progress of the film and secure the necessary approvals along the way.

Marketing a film is very much like producing a film; every step must be considered in order to meet the client's needs as the client sees them. Don't let the term frighten you . . . it's simply a matter of taking care of business.

Filmmakers tend to think of themselves as artists, apart from the clutter of the business world. But no matter how alien the concept of marketing seems, it is still a skill that must be learned and developed. Why? Because marketing is a skill that will help you make the kind of films you want.

"Take that next step beyond your film-making skills . . . business skills don't decrease your freedoms . . . a lot of people are afraid that, 'If I take on business skills, I'm going to spend all my time with tax accounts'; you aren't . . . it means being a little more equipped, more astute, than the next person—doing more than the client expects."

- Filmmakers who learn how to market—how to communicate with clients—are the ones who make films.

- You have nothing to sell, of course, except yourself—and the promise that you can deliver a film that meets your client's needs.

- Don't try for a film that will win prizes. If you try for a film that will best serve your client's needs, you will find yourself with a prizewinner . . . and a recommendation for another job.

- Your reputation is as good as your last film. You build a reputation by taking care of business every day as though your reputation were at stake, because it is.

PART TWO— THE SUCCESSFUL FILM PROPOSAL

WRITING THE PROPOSAL

A successful film proposal is both concise and relevant to everyone who has authority to approve it. It should include the communication objective (the needs to be addressed by the film), a scenario or detailed outline, distribution and promotion plans, and a budget or detailed estimate. It is also a good idea to include a production contract ready for signature. Approval is easier if the proposal is written in terms that are understandable to all concerned. ("SFX" is useful for production purposes, but the term "sound effects" is easier for most people to comprehend; "a film well worth the money" is less relevant than "a way to reach the audience with more impact than a brochure, at a cost of less than $1.50 per person, with a payback in increased performance expected to average $30.00 per person per year.")

Although production and distribution variables are normally worked out before the proposal is written, some—length of the film, location shooting vs studio shooting, number of distribution prints, actor/model choices—may remain at this point. These must be addressed if they are going to affect the perceived quality, acceptance, or cost of the production.

The Communication Objective

A well-written Communication Objective should answer the question, "Why do we need a film in the first place?" The objective is a statement of need and solution. It should pinpoint the usefulness of the proposed film to the client. And it must serve as your guideline throughout the production efforts. If the Communication Objective cannot be stated in a single, short paragraph, it is probably not properly defined.

An ambiguous objective can be costly because you and your client may be thinking different thoughts even when you're speaking the same words. For example, a film designed to help celebrate the centennial of a railroad line might have as its objective "a chronicle of the importance of the railroad in the development of the Pacific Northwest." If your client was a railroad company, that objective—and that film—might work, unless the finished product gave the impression that rail commerce is old fashioned. If it did, you can be sure that your work would never reach an audience. The same project might have a much different perspective if the objective were "a story about the development of the Pacific Northwest and the people who created a modern, progressive railroad." Again, that differs greatly from "a film about a modern, progressive railroad that has its roots in the early development of the Pacific Northwest." You have to realize that you and your clients will often see the same things from different perspectives. That's the reason why your Communication Objective must be clearly stated.

To effectively determine the Communication Objective, you have to understand both your client and your client's audience. Your client may even state a false objective to begin with. You may be working on a film about the history of a company and find out that what the client really wants is a story about the company's product line and sales policies. Your stated objective must be in line with the client's real objectives, and that is part of your job in determining your client's needs. The other half of your decision in writing the Communication Objective comes from your client's audience. Define them. Who are they? What is important to them? Do you know their age, sex, vocational interest, and educational background? What do they know about the subject matter? If you isolate the characteristics of the audience and combine that with the needs of your client, your Communication Objective will be more precise.

The Story Treatment

The story treatment is the "picture" of the proposed production and is usually a scenario—a condensed script—of the film, although a detailed outline can suffice in some cases. However the story is handled, it should effectively convey your solution to your client's needs. It must take into consideration the running time, especially when it is critical, and the budget ceiling, if it is known.

The more explicit your story treatment, the more you will benefit. A detailed, targeted treatment will assist you greatly in determining the precise cost estimate. It will also help your client know what to expect from your production—both how little and how much. The power of words alone can surprise even a sophisticated client. With the specifics in hand, you can itemize your equipment needs, personnel, talent, sets, and any other requirements; you and your client can decide together if the effect is worth the cost.

The Distribution and Promotion Plan

The distribution and promotion phase is, many times, a matter of rote. Many companies have predetermined distribution channels, especially with materials created for internal use (training outlets or salespeople) or for well-established clients (dealers or distributors). You may, however, be able to help your client choose the distribution format. Will the film be shot in 16 mm and converted to 35 mm, then converted back to 16 mm for television use? Will it be shot in 35 mm and converted to 16 mm for distribution? Will it be shot in 16 mm and converted to super-8 format so that salespeople can carry it in a smaller projector to small audiences? Will the same film have several uses in several formats?

Your client's answers will help you determine both the original format and the distribution format, determine costs for the total needs of your client, and avoid serious mistakes when choosing production techniques. A high contrast black-and-white film, for example, might be dramatic in a theatre setting but look muddy or washed out on a television screen. Inadequate planning can ruin even your best work or cause unnecessary costs for your client, and for that reason the distribution format must be considered in your proposal.

Many times, distribution and promotion is the critical point in the decision to make—or not make—a film. Is there an audience for the film? How will you get it to them? How will they know the film is available? These questions must be addressed in the planning stages; and when the answers are not obvious, it is very good business to consult a professional distributor. Distribution and promotion are discussed further in Part Five.

The Budget Breakdown

The distribution plan (and necessary budget) is only one of the vital components of the film proposal; you must also plan and budget for preproduction, production, and postproduction. The object, of course, is to arrive at an accurate estimate of the total costs involved in creating a film and getting it to an audience. This effort requires time and energy. But, without a budget, the details that will come up can be devastating.

The preproduction budget should include expenses for your involvement in preproduction meetings, writing the proposal, and any other planning.

Production expenses are usually the biggest—especially labor; the cost for motion picture film amounts to only about 10 percent of your total budget. Costs are based on the specifics that have been laid out in the story treatment. They include talent, equipment, film, location or studio shooting, sets, transportation, insurances, taxes, and overhead. Thoroughly investigate all potential problem areas in advance, and be aware of time- and money-consuming variables such as weather, creativity, stubbornness, and maybe even some bad luck.

Postproduction is normally more time-consuming than the production process, and the budget costs can be quite substantial. Remember the major areas: film editing, sound effects, optical effects, sound mixing, negative cutting, answer prints, and release prints.

Detailed budget forms—covering preproduction, production, postproduction, and distribution and promotion expenses—are at the end of this chapter.

Samples of Film Proposals

Two examples of complete film proposals are shown on the next few pages. Each example contains a Communication Objective, a Story Treatment, a Distribution and Promotion Plan, and a Budget Estimate of preproduction, production, and postproduction costs.

The first proposal involves a 15-minute animated/live-action film entitled "Rochester, First Person Plural." The client requesting the film is the president of the Rochester, New York, Chamber of Commerce.

The second proposal is for a 30-minute semidocumentary film entitled "The New Field—Grange Farm Enterprise Service." The client is the president of Grange Farm Enterprise, a large farm cooperative.

FILM PROPOSAL SAMPLE—15-MINUTE FILM

Communications Objective

This film is intended to communicate the need for a community-wide approach to problems (education, zoning, housing) that stem from a labor shortage. Emphasis is directed at a "team-effort" from the existing work force, to facilitate the growth and improvement of Rochester.

The client's requirements for the film are: a $12,000 budget ceiling, current aerial still shots (photoanimation) of Rochester, "library" music for background, a professional narrator, and a maximum 10- to 15-minute running time. In addition, the client indicates a preference for: original motion picture aerial footage of Rochester, historical still shots, and high-quality film stock.

Story Treatment
Sequence One

We open with shots of a jet airliner approaching Rochester and move into the cabin to a close-up of one passenger at a window seat. He is a junior executive coming home from a trip. He looks down at the approaching city. We watch subjectively through his eyes, commencing with distant views, then selecting and zeroing in on landmarks that get his attention.

Narration commences, expressing the man's thoughts. His first thoughts are general in nature. "My city—a city with everything going for it with strong, stable industries." The narration becomes more specific and begins to set the stage for discussion of Rochester's labor problems and ideas for their solutions. We move in on the following landmarks:

• A vacant field. This is in a neighboring suburb about which he knows very little, except that his company was planning to build a new facility here—a development that would have opened up new opportunities for his career. However, his company decided to expand out of state.

• A suburban residential development ($40-$50,000 homes). With a sudden shift in pace and mood, the camera turns to the executive's own town. He is proud of it and pleased that it has maintained its distinctive personality. As we focus on the new development, we learn that there was an attempt to use this land for low- and middle-income housing, but it was defeated because of spirited opposition from the townspeople.

• Another shot of the vacant field. The executive wonders why his company decided to build out of state and not expand locally.

Sequence Two

We leave the plane's cabin to show the airliner on final descent and make a transition to artwork, depicting the area as it looked from the air in Rochester's early years. We pick out one house, zoom in on its upper window, and show the view from that window. The narration shows that back in those days—the era of Colonel Nathaniel Rochester—"a man knew his community." He knew that a community was a group of people who shared certain vital interests. A man knew that building the good life for himself and for his family meant more than just keeping up his own house, but also helping to keep the community a good place in which to work. The "greater view" of Rochester, which was exactly what it took to make the town prosper, came naturally.

Sequence Three

We return to the 1970s—quick, candid shots of Rochesterians in different settings—on downtown streets at rush hour, in suburban shopping centers, at parks, at a hockey game, at factories.

The narration states that people haven't changed that much; yet, there are problems. We fill in more details: e.g., a low un-employment rate is not necessarily a sign of health; in fact, it can mean that there is an ominous labor shortage that could stifle growth; that certain services are not being provided with maximum efficiency and that certain changes are needed for a bright future.

Areas to be covered in which a "greater view" is called for will include those in which progress has been made, as well as those in which unification is necessary: zoning, housing, highways and bridges, job training, urban renewal, law enforcement, education, mass transit.

We return to the empty lot and quickly trace the decision of "the company" to locate elsewhere due to a labor shortage. This shortage is attributed to a lack of suitable accommodations within the financial reach of the middle-income work force. This lack of suitable housing is, in turn, traced to unwillingness of individual towns to rezone and provide lower-cost services.

Examples follow to show what this kind of attitude can cost in terms of individual and community dollars:

• Sewage: It takes the same work output and payroll to operate a one-million-gallon-per-day sewage treatment plant as it does to operate a plant with ten times that capacity. Wouldn't it make sense to build fewer and larger plants?

• Highways and Bridges: By the year 2000, the county population will be about 1,350,000 with 313,000 people living in the City of Rochester. The need for arterial roads, and perhaps mass transit, can only be met efficiently through community-wide planning.

• City problems: Expenditures are rising faster than the city's ability to raise taxes. There is an influx of low-income families.

• Job Training: 76 firms and organizations are training people; along with the Chamber of Commerce's guidance, this effort will benefit the entire community.

Narrator says that with vigorous leadership, we have seen a community-wide approach taken to such areas as health, education, welfare, parks, libraries, and museums. These advances suggest the shape of the future and the direction in which our Chamber of Commerce and the community will move.

Narration concludes with a forecast of what Rochester could be in the year 2000 in terms of employment, per-capita income, and general prosperity; "It can be what we all want it to be—a vibrant, happy place in which our children can enjoy a prosperous life. What is needed most is an overall community view that will keep the city on the move." The evolution of this view is a "first person" responsibility—it is also a "plural" responsibility. Narrator says, "If not you, who? If not now, when?"

Running length: 15 minutes, color, sound.

Technique: photographic animation.

Distribution/Promotional Plan: The film will be distributed by the local Public Relations Director of the Rochester Chamber to area public service organizations (e.g., Lions Club, Rotary, Masons). Distribution follows an initial showing of the film to 800 community leaders at the Chamber's annual dinner.

Budget Estimate:

Script to approval draft	$ 1,059.93
Film stock (3-to-1 ratio) figured for 15 minutes finished length (including processing and workprint)	$ 450.00
Still photography, including aerial shots 5 days @ $350.00/day	$ 1,750.00
Aircraft rental, 4 hours	$ 180.00
Narrator and studio	$ 220.00
Library music and studio mix	$ 335.00
Transfer to magnetic stock for analysis and bar-sheeting	$ 50.00
Bar-sheets—setup for 15 minutes	$ 3,150.00
Plotting by director	$ 2,300.00
Photoanimation shooting for 32 hours @ $35.00 per hour	$ 1,120.00
Editing, est. 8 hours @ $35.00	$ 280.00
Timing	$ 200.00
Internegative—540 ft @ .40/ft	$ 216.00
Optical sound track—540 ft @ .18/ft	$ 97.20
Composite answer print—540 ft @ .32/ft	$ 172.80
Grand Total (with script)	$11,580.93

NOTE: All figures are for sample use only.

FILM PROPOSAL SAMPLE—30-MINUTE FILM

Communications Objective

Make it clear to the 30,000 Northeastern U.S. farmers that Grange
Farm Enterprise Service has made available extensive information
analysis resources (e.g., computer assisted techniques); the organization can offer the farmer greater profits and continued independence.
The film will emphasize that Grange is a cooperative, representing
the potential for a close partnership with its progressive farmer
members. The ultimate objective is that the current 10,000-farmer
Grange membership will increase significantly after viewing this film.

   The client's requirements for the film are on-location shooting,
professional talent, and a $40,000 budget ceiling (excluding dis-
tribution costs). The client also indicates a preference for
authentic atmosphere using "wild" farm animal sounds, professionally
made optical titles, and an excellent production crew.

Story Treatment
Sequence One

Scene opens with medium shot of a Northeastern dairy farm at early
dawn. The camera is directed at the lighted farmhouse. Early morning
sounds are heard—cows mooing, a dog barking, and muted voices from
inside the house.

"THE NEW FIELD"

"GRANGE FARM ENTERPRISE SERVICE"

dissolve to:

"A new concept in cooperation
for the needs of agriculture."

   The camera zooms in on the house as the screen door opens; Don
Perkins (a young progressive dairy farmer) steps onto the porch.
(The opening credits are shown on a dark area of the screen.)
Perkins pauses to survey the morning sky, lights his pipe, then
glances at a car passing by on the highway as he starts walking
toward the barn.

   As Perkins walks toward the barn, the camera follows his line of
sight; he gazes at the silo that is looming above the roofline. It is

the type of silo that was standard (and adequate) for dairy farming 10-15 years ago before the major shift to corn feeding. He stops for a moment to assess the silo as his voice-over cuts in: "We'll have to decide about the Grange program pretty soon. Sure as heck will need the help if we get anything like the 25 tons an acre Bill Miller (Grange's sales representative) is talking about. I didn't believe Miller two years ago when the goal was set at 20 tons an acre, but it looks like we'll do better than that this fall. I'm looking for more gallons of milk and less feed costs. Miller will have to help me find out just how much when he brings me some new information."

Perkins has resumed walking toward the barn. He enters the milk parlor, which should be adequate for 80 to 100 milking cows. Perkins' son Tom (about 13) and hired man Carl Peters (about 45) have been milking the cows. Small talk includes a comment by Tom on yesterday's yield of milk—high for this time of year. He questions whether the current tank capacity will be sufficient for next spring's demand. Perkins is quietly amused and pleased at his son's concern and agrees that they may have to add on to their capacity before springtime.

While Tom releases the remaining cows, Carl Peters mentions to Perkins his concern about a cow which they thought had been bred. They go into the barn where the cow is stanchioned and poke the cow in its side. Both agree the cow doesn't appear to be bred. Perkins is mystified. This is the third or fourth such breeding failure in the past six months. Peters comments on the money that they lose from such failures. Their voices go under.

The narrator's voice comes over as the men continue their morning activities. The narration points out that farming today is an increasingly complex, competitive, high-volume/low-margin business. It is no longer enough to be just good; you have to be big and growing bigger to meet the rising break-even points that characterize today's farming economy. (Visuals for these comments could include shots of milk storage tanks, automatic pipeline cleaning equipment, and conveyorized feeding equipment.)

The narrator continues by saying that a staggering amount of inputs affect farming on a daily basis — 10,000 scientists and researchers pouring out reports and findings. How can the individual farmer hope to analyze and digest it all? The answer is that the farmer really can't (during the conclusion of these remarks, the camera zooms from an overall shot to a strong triangular shape, such as a triangular window at the end of the hay mow).

Sequence Two

(Dissolve from the triangular window to an "A" shape of Perkins' barn frame. Zooms, pans, and cuts to artwork and photographs follow, to be accomplished with photoanimation.) The narrator continues: a pooling of strength to accomplish what the individual cannot do alone is a tradition of American agriculture (zoom back to show a barn-building scene). During the earliest group efforts of barn-building, silo filling, and crew thrashing, farmers made use of their collective strengths to secure supplies of certified, reliable seed. Farmers then established open-feed formulas and better price levels through cooperative buying and marketing (visuals show animation of old photos: "better seed societies," the first buying and marketing co-ops).

Each successful collective venture improved some individual aspect of the farmer's situation—prices paid for feed or seed, prices received for milk or produce. However, the new challenge to agriculture today is much more complex; not just milk from a cow (animation of still photo—cow-milking) but the best possible milk from today's dairy animal (dissolve to a scene of a modern milking parlor). In today's farming, "corn from a field" will not keep you in business . . . (shot of mid-thirties corn harvester and typical corn stand). Today's narrow farming margins demand the best-quality corn at the lowest possible cost.

The challenge to today's agriculture is for optimum efficiency in the management of all farm-enterprise resources: commodities, labor, land, buildings, and capital (visuals to cover modern facilities of progressive farm operations).

What is necessary is a marshalling of talent in all major agricultural fields, including agronomy, animal nutrition, herd health and sanitation, farm structures and material handling, and even farming expenses such as insurance and petroleum services. Tailoring best-choice solutions to individual farm situations requires the latest techniques and tools of management science and information technology, including electronic data processing (supported by glimpses of activity in labs, offices, data processing rooms).

(Cut to artwork of barn-building) The challenge today is as far beyond the capabilities of the individual farmer as it was years ago to raise and set a three-ton barn frame. This is a new-but-classic reason for farmers to pool their strength—to accomplish through cooperation a vital task they cannot accomplish alone.

Grange Farm Enterprise Service is the total mobilization of Grange know-how—combined with new tools and techniques of management science and information technology—to help you achieve the efficient resource management that is essential for success and survival in farming today (camera zooms back to show some of the "mobilized" resources at Grange headquarters: lab facilities, personnel, and communications gear. The final view shows an over-all shot of Grange headquarters in Springfield, followed by a zoom-in on the Grange logo at the top of the building).

Sequence Three

Narration continues: The Grange Farm Enterprise facility offers everyday products and conveniences to its members. Its place of availability (a noticeable change in lighting on the Grange logo that is still filling the screen) is the local Grange store that you have always patronized (camera zooms back to show that a new Grange sign is on a representative local outlet). The counselor who will make the expanding resources of Grange Farm Enterprise Service available to you is your local Grange salesperson, such as Bill Miller (camera moves in-store to show Miller getting ready for a day's calls). But nowadays Miller has a new title and a new assignment.

- The new title is "Grange Enterprise Service Representative."
- His new assignment is to have a full working knowledge of every information-analysis resource and to urge the farmer to take fullest advantage of modern services to make the farm enterprise more profitable. This assignment takes precedence over the sale of Grange's goods and services.

Bill Miller is dedicated to the maximum success of your farm; that is as it always has been. Over the past several months, he has been heavily involved with new training programs in Springfield called Enterprise Profile Services. The objective is to upgrade and improve the efficiency of virtually every aspect of the farming operation (during these comments, Miller is shown sorting various Profile reports).

Consider, for instance, this Least-Cost Grain Profile for dairyman Mike Corrigan (camera zooms in on report). The narrator explains that this is an analysis of Powers' own home-grown grains in successive combination with fourteen commercially available rations. The least-cost formula offers a difference of four cents in income over feed costs per cow per day. It does not sound like much, but pennies are making the difference between success and failure in today's farming. Four cents times 100 cows times 305 days equals $1200 a year.

The narrator points out that a number of calculations are necessary to arrive at a least-cost formula at ten production levels, four protein levels, and three TDN levels (show a close-up of the Grain Profile). The narrator goes on to say that this individualized service is possible only through the use of computer services and the know-how of Grange's programming experts (appropriate scenes of EDP facilities in Springfield). The emphasis is on the computer's enormous talent for refining information and defining alternatives; but the final decision is still the farmer-manager's. The farmer-member can rent the service of an IBM 360 computer for as little as $2.50 per week; it could prove to be the most important "farm implement" since the combine.

The narrator explains that through the use of computer facilities in Springfield, the Enterprise Representative can offer least-cost formulations or performance analysis for all major areas of farm operation, including (quick cuts to appropriate visuals): monthly and year-to-date dairy herd profiles, dairy and group feeding profiles, herd health and sanitation, crop programs, automation plans, poultry program, swine systems, beef systems, fruit programs, members insurance service, and complete petroleum services. (Each of the foregoing is briefly explained and visualized with references to results already realized. The point can be made here that profile programs work best along with Grange products because their values are known and certified).

(The camera returns to the Grange Store and Bill Miller. Action centers on Miller's final preparations to leave for a day's rounds). The narration concludes with a statement that Miller has a great deal more in his briefcase than order forms. The value of the analysis and consulting services (Miller is now qualified to offer) is realized by him with each passing day's calls on the farmer-members.

Sequence Four

There is a transition to live dialogue between Miller and the Grange store manager. The conversation reveals that Grange representative Miller will make a call on a dairyman named Bob Martin. The manager's comments make it clear that this is apt to be an unrewarding experience for Miller. The impression is that Martin is unprogressive and uncooperative. There is reference to a Grain Profile that Miller will discuss with Mike Corrigan and a Corn Program and Farm Resource Profile for Don Perkins. (It is learned through good-humored teasing between Miller and the store manager that Miller gave up smoking several months ago—he pops a Lifesaver into his mouth whenever the urge hits for a cigarette.)

Miller enters his car. As he drives along rural roads to his first call to see dairyman Bob Martin, the following points of interest provoke these voice-over thoughts:

• A Mercedes-Benz is parked at the former Ducolon farm. The

farmhouse and other buildings are in poor shape. Miller's
thoughts reveal that this is now a "gentleman's farm" formerly
belonging to a farmer who wanted to keep the herd and facilities
at a 30- to 35-cow level. "In today's farming, it's grow or go."

• Miller observes an alfalfa field that is well on its way
toward a fourth cutting. He would not have believed this to be
possible in the Northeast as recently as six or seven years ago.
There is a quick flashback to the Grange Enterprise training
session that Miller attended in Springfield. He recalls his
growing enthusiasm upon learning of the resources already
marshalled in support of the Enterprise objectives.

• Miller anticipates the reception that he will get at
Martin's place. Through flashbacks we learn that:
    (a) Martin regards him as no more than a "feed peddler."
    (b) Martin is backward about keeping the type of records that
effective management demands. Miller knows that he will find a
new shipment of "bargain" feed in Martin's barn. He feels Martin
cannot grasp the idea that Grange's ability to help its members
make a profit far outweighs its role of helping the farmer save
money on purchases of grain.
    (c) Martin is suspicious of any requests for information that
relate to his income, expenses, or finances.
    (d) Finally, Miller ponders about the sense of
"independence." He speculates that Martin has not distinguished
between good, helpful intentions and "meddling."

Miller's car pulls into Martin's place. A large dog jumps along-
side the driver's side, barking aggressively. Martin appears at the
barn door and shouts, "I'll be damned if that dog can't smell a feed
peddler half a mile away." (Close-up of Miller's face.) It's going
to be a long morning. (Fade-out)

Sequence Five

(Dissolve: back to Miller looking up at the sky. It's now a
different lighting arrangement and obviously a different time setting

and situation; zoom back to show that Perkins is standing beside Miller.) They are talking about the new grain silo (its early stages of construction) and a conveyor system. Perkins is pleased that their predicted amortization period is shorter than he had imagined and says that he hopes to have the most valuable farm around.

Miller and Perkins walk back toward the dooryard through the barn. Perkins calls Miller's attention to the "dry" cow that was shown in the opening sequence. Miller confirms that the cow is not pregnant. They both speculate on the problem. Miller asks Perkins if he has a recent Dairy-Group Feeding Profile. Perkins good-naturedly remarks that Miller has found a good reason to get into Miller's house, and coincidentally, at dinnertime. Miller agrees, "this is especially nice since it's cherry-picking season and there may be a cherry pie in the house."

(Cut: to Perkin's dining room.) We meet Perkins' wife, Eileen. She gets the Feeding Profile and joins the men to review it. There is reference to a recommended $2100 increase in feed costs that had returned $2800 in income beyond the feed costs. Then, Miller's attention fixes on a calcium-phosphorus ratio that shows the phosphorus to be under the recommended levels; he speculates that this could be part of the problem. Eileen Perkins recalls reading of such a situation in the Farm Journal. Miller offers to look into the problem with the Springfield office and suggests an immediate mineral supplement program. Perkins states that Miller may have earned his dinner. Eileen mentions that a large wedge of cherry pie is waiting for Miller on the table. (Dissolve)

Sequence Six

(Dissolve: back to a scene of farewells at Perkins' doorway.) It is getting dark. Miller is now in his car talking with Perkins. He remarks about the Mercedes-Benz he saw at the former Ducolon farm. Miller has heard that the new owner's permanent home is in Connecticut and observes that it would take quite a few "milk checks" to buy a car like that. Perkins agrees, then comments, "But I

don't have to spend my Sunday afternoons driving around looking
for a farm. I've already got one." There are parting comments
about Miller's intention to check with the Springfield office on
the low-phosphorus problem. Perkins admits that he intends to take
the Farm Resource Profile for his new silo to the bank to help
justify financing the silo. Perkins jokingly speculates that the
bank should let him build a football stadium on his property if he
would provide the bank with a favorable Resource Profile. (Final
farewells.)

(Cut: Miller driving in his car.) He appears mildly distraught
and pops a Lifesaver in his mouth. He is held up at Martin's farm;
Martin is guiding his cows across the road. (Voice-over follows—
Miller is talking to himself.) "Friend, somehow I'm going to be
working for you or else I'm afraid you may end up working in another
line of business." Miller and Martin exchange genuine, friendly
waves.

(Cut: back to Perkins' farm; he's still standing in his doorway.)
He goes onto the porch, lights his pipe, and then looks at the
location where his silo will be in the spring. His voice comes over,
"Guess we won't need any parking space for a Mercedes-Benz around here
for awhile." (Camera zooms back—continuing to center on Perkins—
until we approximate the nature of the story's opening scene.)
The screen door opens and Tom comes out to see what his father is
doing. They go back into the kitchen where Eileen Perkins can be
seen doing after-dinner chores.

On a dark area of the screen, the following quotation is superimposed:

"If agriculture is to continue to prosper under a democratic
form of government, or if we are to be a nation of the free men
of the soil, then we must organize our industry—that means
cooperation."

Dean Beverly T. Galloway
Cornell University, 1915

Dissolve to end credits.

Music Up

Running Length: 30 minutes—shot for TV cutoff.

Technique: Color; live action and animated still photography.

Distribution/Promotional Plan:

The film will be shown (via the Grange Farm Enterprise Public Relations Department) to all present farm cooperative members. To reach the farmers who are not Grange members, the film will be aired on the local PBS television station—slotted for a Sunday afternoon. A press release will be sent to the local newspapers which will announce the day and time of the broadcast.

Budget Estimate:

1. Script to approval draft .... $ 3,300.00
2. Crew—including director, production manager,
   cameras, lighting, grips, and gaffers.
   Estimated 4 days @ $2,500 a day $10,000.00
3. Scouting time: 2 people guaranteed .... $ 450.00
4. Optical titles from subcontractor .... $ 800.00
5. Sound technician, extra for wild sounds .... $ 500.00
6. Film stock (including processing)—to workprint .... $ 3,196.00
7. Talent .... $ 6,200.00
8. Additional location dressing (groundskeeping,
   repair, painting) .... $ 1,200.00
9. Farm animals, additional shipment .... $ 1,400.00
10. Props (rent and build) .... $ 4,500.00
11. Completion, to approved answer print—including all
    editing, sound mixing, opticals .... $ 6,200.00
                 Grand Total (with script) $37,746.00

NOTE: All figures are for sample use only.

PREPARING THE FILM BUDGET

Overestimating can cost you the job; underestimating can cost you money. "Creative" estimating causes ulcers; accurate estimating happens because you're thoroughly knowledgeable in the details of motion picture production and also a little bit lucky. As a filmmaker, you must be aware of the variables that exist. You're winning one day when you finish shooting ahead of schedule, but you're losing another when the effects come back all wrong.

Many filmmakers try to cover the unpredictable with contingency budgeting. With contingency budgeting, you add 10 to 20 percent to the total budget just in case things go wrong. If everything works as planned, you come in under budget and you're a hero to your client; if the worst happens, you come in on budget and nobody knows how you have sweated. In any case, you should warn your client that it is possible for the project to go beyond the initial estimate. Some causes for budget alterations are union strikes, illness of talent or crew, equipment malfunction, or poor weather during location shootings.

You can only hope to create a reasonably accurate budget after you have taken a realistic look at everything required to put your ideas on film. We are offering two types of budget forms for your consideration:

The first—the short form shown on the next page—covers the details that are usually encountered in nontheatrical filmmaking. Start with this form when you create your own budgeting forms.

The longer forms shown on pages 31 through 47 involve detailed lists of items normally considered for theatricals. We include them because they may be helpful in determining costs for uncommonly complex nontheatrical productions.

More important than following forms is recognizing the many details involved in producing a film. Do yourself and your client a favor: Think the film all the way through—from preproduction through distribution—before you submit a budget for approval.

MOTION PICTURE ESTIMATE SHEET

Date of Estimate _____

Project Number	Project Title				Project Manager	
Client Contact				Target Date	Estimator	

LABOR CATEGORIES	PEOPLE	HRS	RATE	DOLLARS	MATERIAL & SERVICES CATEGORIES	DOLLARS
Research					Raw stock/workprint/process	
Writing					Magnetic tape & film	
Production Planning					Props rent/buy	
Casting & Loc. Sel.					Equip. usage fees	
Set Const. & Dress					Set costs	
Travel					Travel & Subsistence	
Photography					Actors	
Title Photography					Narrators	
Sound Record & Trans.					Producers	
Mix—M & E					Writers	
Editing					Motion Picture Photographers	
Review Rushes					Misc. outside services	
Post Direction					Film contracts	
Rewrite & Narrate					Audio Services	
Music Selection					Music/license	
Client Review					Titles/artwork	
Pull & Match Orig.					Optical lab work/masters	
Stand By					Sound Track Negative	
Strike Set					Answer Print	
Miscellaneous					Release Prints	
Filing & Clean Up						
Sub Total						
Contingency						

Fixed Cost ☐ Yes ☐ No

Length _____ Emul # _____ Shooting Ratio _____ 1

Contingency	
Total Material & Service	
Total Labor Cost	
Total Project Cost	

Remarks _____

_____

_____

_____

_____

SCRIPT (Account Number 1): A typical practice is to charge ten percent of the total budget to the script. You may not be able to obtain the services of a professional scriptwriter for that percentage; however, if you hire a beginning (yet competent) writer, his or her fee could fall *under* the ten percent rate.

CONTINUITY AND TREATMENT (Account Number 2): This account refers to administrative costs for script preparation and handling. All expenses for script research, secretarial work, and duplicating are part of this account.

PRODUCER AND DIRECTOR (Account Numbers 3 and 4): In nontheatrical (documentary, industrial, sponsored) films, the producer often performs double-duty as the director of the production. On the other hand, directors of television commercial productions are recognized as very specialized (and thus costly) people capable of making major contributions. The range of fees for these two accounts can vary depending on union affiliation.

Film Title _____ Picture No. _____

Date Prepared _____

Account Number	Description	Days, Weeks, or Quantity	Rate	Totals
1	SCRIPT			
A	—Script Purchase			
	TOTAL STORY			
2	CONTINUITY AND TREATMENT			
A	—Writers			
B	—Secretary			
C	—Duplication			
D	—Research Expense			
	TOTAL CONTINUITY AND TREATMENT			
3	PRODUCER			
A	—Producer			
B	—Asst. Producer			
C	—Secretaries			
	TOTAL PRODUCER			
4	DIRECTOR			
A	—Director			
B	—Secretaries			
	TOTAL DIRECTORS			

CAST (Account Number 5): Bad casting creates unwanted, costly problems. Whether you use professional actors or nonprofessional actors you should conduct a thorough selection process. Some of the ways in which you can contact actors are through casting companies, open casting, talent agents in film and television, daily contacts, and community theatres. Open casting involves your own public announcement that you are holding auditions for a film. Interview the prospective talents with help from the casting director, whose services are invaluable in the final selection of cast members and negotiation for their fees. (This account calls out the word "buyout." A buyout refers to a film contract with a nonunion talent for a *one-time* fee.)

BITS AND EXTRAS (Account Numbers 6 and 7): Bits and extras are usually paid according to the union scale. Bits and extras in a production can substantially increase a film's impact, depending on the subject and its treatment. There are some excellent actors who only perform bits (small parts) in a film.

Title _____ Picture No. _____

Date Prepared _____

Account Number	Description	Days, Weeks, or Quantity	Rate	Totals
5	CAST			
	Buyouts			
	Pension			
	Contributions			
	TOTAL CAST			
6	BITS			
	Buyouts			
	Pension			
	Contributions			
	Overtime on Bits			
	TOTAL BITS			
7	EXTRAS			
	Overtime for Extras			
	Service Fees for Extras			
	Adjustments for Extras			
	Stand-ins			
	School Teacher(s)			
	Stunt People			
	Stunt Adjustments			
	Buyouts			
	Pensions			
	Contributions			
	TOTAL EXTRAS			

PRODUCTION STAFF (Account Numbers 8 and 9): The production staff should be carefully selected by the producer. If the staff consists of union personnel you will be required to employ a minimum number, depending on requirements established by the union. A well-integrated, skillful crew can cut down on your production time and significantly reduce your costs.

Title		Picture No.			
		Date Prepared			

Account Number	Description	Days, Weeks, or Quantity	Rate		Totals
8	PRODUCTION STAFF				
	SALARIES				
A	—Production Mgr.				
B	—Unit Manager				
C	—1st Asst. Director				
	Severance				
D	—2nd Asst. Director				
	Severance				
E	—Extra Asst. Dir.				
F	—Dialogue Clerk				
G	—Script Clerk				
H	—Dance Director				
I	—Casting Director				
	and Staff				
J	—Technical Advisor				
K	—First Aid				
L	—Location Auditor				
M	—Secretaries				
	TOTAL PRODUCTION				
	STAFF				
9	PRODUCTION OPERATING				
	STAFF				
	A-Camera Operator				
1	—1st Camera Oper.				
2	—Camera Operators				
3	—Focus Asst.				
	Camera Oper.				
4	—Asst. Camera Oper.				
5	—Camera Mechanics				
6	—Color Director				
7	—Still Person				
8	—Still Gaffer				
9	—Process Cam. Oper.				
10	—Asst. Process				
	Camera Operator				
11	—Extra Camera Oper.				
12	—Extra Camera Asst.				
13	—O.T. Camera Crew				
	TOTAL ACCT 9-A				

Account Number	Description	Days, Weeks, or Quantity	Rate	Totals	
9	PRODUCTION OPERATING				
	STAFF (cont'd)				
	B-Sound Dept.				
1	—Mixer				
2	—Recorder				
3	—Boom Person				
4	—Cable Person				
5	—Cable Boom Person				
6	—P.A. System Oper.				
7	—Sound Effects Person				
8	—Sound Maintenance				
	TOTAL ACCT 9-B				
	C-Wardrobe Dept.				
1	—Wardrobe Designer				
2	—Wardrobe Buyer				
3	—1st Wardrobe Girl				
4	—2nd Wardrobe Girl				
5	—1st Wardrobe Man				
6	—2nd Wardrobe Man				
7	—Tailor				
8	—Seamstress				
9	—Extra Help				
	TOTAL ACCT 9-C				
	D-Makeup and				
	Hairdressing				
1	—Head Makeup Person				
2	—2nd Makeup Person				
3	—Head Hairdresser				
4	—2nd Hairdresser				
5	—Body Makeup Girl				
6	—Extra Help				
	TOTAL ACCT 9-D				

Title _____   Picture No. _____

Date Prepared _____

		Title		Picture No.			

Title _____ Picture No. _____

Date Prepared _____

Account Number	Description	Days, Weeks, or Quantity	Rate		Totals	
9	PRODUCTION OPERATING					
	STAFF (cont'd)					
	E-Grip Dept.					
1	—1st Grip					
2	—Best Boy					
3	—Set Operation					
	Grips					
4	—Extra Labor					
5	—Camera Boom Oper.					
6	—Crab Dolly Grip					
	TOTAL ACCT 9-E					
	F-Property Dept.					
1	—Head Property Person					
2	—2nd Property Person					
3	—3rd Property Person					
4	—Outside Help					
5	—Extra Help					
	TOTAL ACCT 9-F					
	G-Set Dressing Dept.					
1	—Head Set Dresser					
2	—Asst. Set Dresser					
3	—Swing Gang					
4	—Drapery Person					
5	—Asst. Drapery Person					
6	—Nursery Person					
7	—Extra Labor					
	TOTAL ACCT 9-G					
	H-Electrical Dept.					
1	—Gaffer					
2	—Best Boy					
3	—Elect Op. Labor					
4	—Generator Op.					
5	—Elect. Maint. Person					
6	—Wind Machine Op.					
	TOTAL ACCT 9-H					

Title			Picture No.		
			Date Prepared		

Account Number	Description	Days, Weeks, or Quantity	Rate	Totals
9	PRODUCTION OPERATING			
	STAFF (cont'd)			
	I-Labor Dept.			
1	—Standby Laborer			
2	—Asst. Laborers			
	TOTAL ACCT 9-I			
	J-Special Effects			
1	—Head Spec. Eff. Person			
2	—Asst. Spec. Eff. Person			
	TOTAL ACCT 9-J			
	K-Set Standby Oper.			
1	—Carpenter			
	TOTAL ACCT 9-K			
	L-Set Standby Painters			
	TOTAL ACCT 9-L			
	M-Set Watch Person			
1	—Watch Person			
	TOTAL ACCT 9-M			
	N-Wranglers			
1	—S.P.C.A. Person			
2	—Head Wrangler			
3	—Wranglers			
	O-Miscellaneous			
	GRAND TOTAL PROD.			
	OPERATING SALARIES			

SET CONSTRUCTION AND OPERATION EXPENSES (Account Numbers 10 and 11): The modern-day production is best carried out on location for maximum realism and presence. Productions that have scenes with extensive dialogue are often more effectively produced at the studio. The production budget should also dictate the amount and type of equipment required. Minor yet essential pieces of equipment are occasionally left out of the budget. For example, the script may indicate the need for an extreme closeup; thus, you'll need a telephoto lens.

Title		Picture No.		
		Date Prepared		

Account Number	Description	Days, Weeks, or Quantity	Rate	Totals
10	SET CONSTRUCTION			
A	—Art Director			
B	—Asst. Art Director			
C	—Sketch Artist			
D	—Draftsman			
E	—Set Supervisor			
F	—Material and Supplies			
G	—Construction Supervisor			
H	—Miscellaneous			
	TOTAL SETS			

Title _____ Picture No. _____

Date Prepared _____

Account Number	Description	Days, Weeks, or Quantity	Rate	Totals
11	SET OPERATION EXPENSES			
A	—Camera Equipment Rentals			
B	—Camera Equipment Purchases			
C	—Camera Car Rentals			
D	—Camera Crane Rentals			
E	—Wardrobe Purchased			
F	—Wardrobe Rentals			
G	—Wardrobe Mainten.			
H	—Grip Equip. Rented			
I	—Prop Equip. Rented			
J	—Props Purchased			
JJ	—Prop Person's Petty Cash Exp.			
K	—Props Rented			
L	—Props—Loss and Damage			
M	—Set Dressing Rentals			
N	—Set Dressing Purchased			
O	—Draperies Purchased and Rented			
P	—Makeup Purchases			
Q	—Hairdressing Purchases & Rentals			
R	—Elect. Equip. Rentals			
S	—Elect. Equip. Purch.			
T	—Elect. Power			
U	—Rentals on Picture Cars-Trucks-Planes			
V	—Misc. Rentals & Purch.			
W	—Special Effect —Purch. & Rentals			
	TOTAL SET OPERATION EXPENSE			

CUTTING FILM LAB (Account Number 12): Cutting film lab expenses fall in the postproduction area. After the shooting is completed, your film is still subject to considerably more work before it's in the can. The workprint will be edited; sound effects will be put into sound tracks; music will be scored and edited to a workprint; and all separate sound tracks (music, narration, sound effects, and dialogue) must be combined onto one track. Titling and special optical effects come into play. The negative must be cut and matched to the workprint. The laboratory will finally make the composite answer prints. Since costs for these services can fluctuate from lab to lab, you should obtain a firm price quote and carefully assess the results against the "knowns" of quality, service, and delivery.

Title			Picture No.		
			Date Prepared		

Account Number	Description	Days, Weeks, or Quantity	Rate		Totals	
12	CUTTING FILM LAB					
A	—Editor					
B	—Asst. Cutter					
C	—Sound Cutter					
D	—Music Cutter					
E	—Negative Cutter					
	TOTAL LABOR					
F	—Negative Action Raw Stock					
G	—Negative Sound Raw Stock					
GG	—Tape Rental					
H	—Develop Action					
HH	—Develop Sound					
I	—Print Action					
II	—Print Sound					
J	—Magnastrip Proc.					
JJ	—Magnastrip Score and Dubbing					
K	—Color Scene Pilot Strips					
KK	—16 mm Color Prints					
KKK	—Internegative					
L	—Separation Masters					
LL	—Interpositive					
M	—Answer Print					
MM	—Composite Print					
N	—Fine Grain Print					
NN	—Panchromatic					
NNN	—16 mm Prints					
O	—Fades-Dissolves-Dupes & Fine Grain					
OO	—Reprints					
P	—Titles, Main/End					
Q	—Cutting Room Rental					
R	—Coding or Edge Numbering					

Title _____   Picture No. _____
                             Date Prepared _____

Account Number	Description	Days, Weeks, or Quantity	Rate		Totals	
12	CUTTING FILM LAB					
	(cont'd)					
RR	—Projection					
S	—Editing Machine Rentals					
T	—Reels & Leader					
U	—Cutting Room Supplies					
	TOTAL CUTTING FILM LAB					

MUSIC AND SOUND (Account Numbers 13 and 14): The need for music and sound track services will vary depending on your particular production. To employ *prerecorded* sound (thereby lowering the costs) generally results in only satisfactory quality. Original renditions of custom sound, however, are highly recommended and proportionately more expensive. Some producers obtain single-instrument improvisational music, secure an original sound recording, and save money in the long run.

TRANSPORTATION, LOCATION, AND STUDIO RENTAL (Account Numbers 15, 16, and 17): Costs for transportation, location, and studio rental are often buried some place in the production budget. These expenses should not be treated as such, because clients, sponsors, and investors will generally expect and deserve to see complete and accurate estimates.

Title _____   Picture No. _____

Date Prepared _____

Account Number		Description	Days, Weeks, or Quantity	Rate		Totals	
13		MUSIC					
	A	—Music Supervisor					
	B	—Director					
	C	—Composer					
	D	—Musicians					
	D	—Singers					
	F	—Arrangers					
	G	—Copyists					
	H	—Royalties					
	I	—Purchases					
	J	—Miscellaneous					
	K	—Instrument Rental and Shipment					
	L	—Librarian					
		TOTAL MUSIC					
14		SOUND					
	A	—Royalties					
	B	—Dubbing Room Rental					
	C	—Pre-Score Equip. Rentals					
	D	—Scoring Equipment Rentals					
	E	—Labor for Dubbing					
	F	—Sound Equipment Rentals					
		TOTAL SOUND					
15		TRANSPORTATION STUDIO					
	A	—Labor					
	B	—Car Rentals					
	C	—Truck Rentals					
	D	—Bus Rentals					
	E	—Car Allowance					
	F	—Gas & Oil—Mileage					

TESTS AND RETAKES (Account Number 18): These potential expenses fall in the contingency budgeting area. For example, you may encounter a talent who decides to quit the production in midstream. You are now faced with having to hire another person and thus an additional unexpected cost. Cover yourself and allow for surprises. (The tests and retakes account does not include unforeseen personal accidents on the set. Insurance for accidents and mishaps is covered in Account Number 21.)

Title		Picture No.		
		Date Prepared		

Account Number	Description	Days, Weeks, or Quantity	Rate	Totals
16	LOCATION			
A	—Traveling			
B	—Hotel			
C	—Lodging			
D	—Location Sites Rental			
E	—Special Equipment			
F	—Car Rentals			
G	—Bus Rentals			
H	—Truck Rentals			
I	—Sundry Employees			
J	—Location Office Rental			
K	—Gratuities			
L	—Miscellaneous			
M	—Scouting & Pre-Production			
N	—Police Services and Permits			
O	—Contact Person			
	TOTAL LOCATION			
17	STUDIO RENTALS			
A	—Stage Space			
B	—Street Rentals			
C	—Test			
D	—Vacation Allowance (studio)			
E	—Surcharge on Rentals and Studio Charges			
F	—Miscellaneous Exp.			
G	—Portable Dressing Rooms			
H	—Office Rentals			
	TOTAL STUDIO RENTALS			
18	TESTS & RETAKES			
A	—Tests Prior to Production			
B	—Tests During Production			

Title		Picture No.			
		Date Prepared			

Account Number	Description	Days, Weeks, or Quantity	Rate	Totals	
18	TESTS & RETAKES				
	(cont'd)				
C	—Retakes after				
	Principal Photo				
D	—Preproduction				
	Expense/Sheeting				
	TOTAL TESTS & RETAKES				

PUBLICITY (Account Number 19): Efficient publicity for your film is important. Advertising helps you build a good client/producer relationship, and can also be applied to promotion of a film. While it is not standard practice to note the publicity costs directly within the budget, your client should be reminded that this area is of the utmost importance to the success of the project.

MISCELLANEOUS (Account Number 20): Miscellaneous costs also fall in the contingency realm. Review your plan and the script for all expected costs that may not even be indicated on any of these budgeting forms.

INSURANCE, TAXES, LICENSE AND FEES (Account Number 21): All production personnel and equipment should be protected by insurance. The risks are greater when you are shooting in remote locations or in areas where wide temperature variations are extreme enough to cause concern for raw film stock damage. Also, be prepared for personal property taxes (if you own a studio), city or county licenses (e.g., permission to shoot at someone's place of business), and any other fees that may crop up on location.

Title _____ Picture No. _____

Date Prepared _____

Account Number	Description	Days, Weeks, or Quantity	Rate	Totals
19	PUBLICITY			
A	—Advertising			
B	—Unit Publicity Person			
C	—Entertainment			
D	—Trade/Newspaper Subscriptions			
E	—Publicity Stills Salaries			
F	—Publicity Stills Supplies			
G	—Publicity Stills Lab Charges			
H	—Still Gallery Rental/Expense			
I	—Trailer			
J	—Press Preview Exp.			
K	—Supplies Postage & Express			
L	—Miscellaneous			
	TOTAL PUBLICITY			
20	MISCELLANEOUS			
A	—Vacation Allowance			
B	—Retroactive Wage Contingency			
C	—Sundry Unclassified Expense			
D	—Set Beverages			
E	—Water & Ice			
	TOTAL MISCELLANEOUS			
21	INSURANCE, TAXES, LICENSE & FEES			
A	—Cast Insurance			
B	—Life Insurance			
C	—Misc. Insurance			
D	—Compensation & Public Liab. Ins.			
E	—Soc. Sec. Tax			
F	—Negative Stock Insurance			

Title		Picture No.				
		Date Prepared				

Account Number	Description	Days, Weeks, or Quantity	Rate		Totals	
21	INSURANCE, TAXES,					
	LICENSE & FEES (cont'd)					
G	—Personal Prop. Tax					
H	—Misc. Taxes/License					
I	—City Tax/License					
J	—Health & Welfare					
	Contribution					
K	—Pension Plan—					
	Crafts					
	TOTAL ACCT 21					

GENERAL OVERHEAD (Account Number 22): General overhead costs are not to be included under miscellaneous expenses because they are a distinct budget element. This area generally includes your administrative personnel, office supplies, and telephone bills. Review the list provided here and make required modifications to suit your needs.

Title		Picture No.		
		Date Prepared		

Account Number	Description	Days, Weeks, or Quantity	Rate	Totals
22	GENERAL OVERHEAD			
A	—Flat Charge			
B	—Corporate Overhead Expense			
C	—Casting Office Salaries			
D	—Entertainment— Executives			
E	—Travel Expense— Executives			
F	—Office Rental and Expense			
G	—Auditor			
H	—Timekeeper			
I	—Secretaries			
J	—Public Relations Head			
K	—Public Relations Secretary			
L	—Legal Fees			
M	—Office Supplies			
N	—Postage—Telephone & Telegraph			
O	—Customs Brokerage			
P	—Contingency			
Q	—General Office			
R	—Film Shipping			
	TOTAL GENERAL OVERHEAD			

DISTRIBUTION (Account Number 23): Although the determination of the distribution costs is not strictly the producer's responsibility, this area should be reviewed with the client. Distribution arrangements are not exactly the same for every film. If the production is a documentary-type film, you should locate distribution companies that specialize in this field. There are also distributors that handle sponsored films, educational films, corporate-informational films, and television-syndicated productions. If costs are critical and you cannot afford a distributor's fee, consider self-distribution of the film, which will require initial advertising in the public media.

Title _____ Picture No. _____

Date Prepared _____

Account Number		Description	Days, Weeks, or Quantity	Rate		Totals
23		DISTRIBUTION				
	A	—Prints				
	B	—Literature &				
		Printed Promo.				
	C	—Print Maint.				
	D	—Postage/Shipping				
	E	—Correspondence				
		(secretarial)				
	F	—Customs/Duties				
	G	—Insurance				
	H	—Miscellaneous Costs				
		TOTAL DISTRIBUTION				

SECURING THE PRODUCTION CONTRACT

Signing the production contract is the last and most vital step before you begin production. After you and your client have signed a contract, there is no room for error. The contract constitutes a legally binding agreement. You should not begin any production work until your client has signed that contract.

Ask your client to sign the contract within 60 days after you have submitted it. This action can help you avoid a period of "limbo." Certainly it will take some time for approvals from your client. But the longer the contract is idle, the longer you risk losing a job with another prospective client. Be sure that the contract includes the total price for the job, required deadline dates, conditions for ownership of the film, and a provision for breaking the contract under an extreme case.

The sample contract that follows is very basic and is typical for an industrial or documentary film; it is provided for illustrative purposes only. Accompanying the contract is a list of eight general provisions that should be included. Get legal assistance for preparing your own production contracts, particularly if you have never written one.

Production Contract
(your) Film Company

Job No.: _____
Date: _____

Client: _____   Producer: _____
Product: _____   Proposal Due: _____
Film Identification: _____   Job No.: _____
_____   Your P.O. No.: _____

FILM PRODUCTION SPECIFICATIONS (circle appropriate items)

No. of release prints; release quantity; optical; b&w; color stock

format prints: rev., pos., anim., supers.

_____   shooting:

wild foot. loc. studio; sync sound loc. studio;   b&w   color   loc.   studio
wild sound loc. studio

_____   narration system:

No. of items enclosed   outlines v/o   on-cam.   other

storyboards   synopses   scripts

RESPONSIBILITY FOR REQUIREMENTS

C: provided by client   P: provided by producer
OK: to be approved by client   Due: date

	C	P	OK	Due		C	P	OK	Due
script					director				
storyboard					director (asst.)				
set design					product tests				
set construction					production mtg.				
props					production bkd.				
prop person					production sched.				
client product					shooting sched.				
prep. of 7 for cam.					camera sequence				
location search					set call				
casting					location fees				
costumes					special effects				
studio facilities					still photos				
direct of photog.					expenses—living				
narration record					crew				
narrator					agency				
narration direct					transportation—				
singers					crew				
name talent					talent				
music library					agency				
music arrangement					reservat.				
music fees					insurance—film				
talent fees					insurance—liab.				
talent releases					lighting equip.				
technical advisor					lighting tech.				
makeup					grip				
art direction					script girl				
art/title					cinematographer				
finished art					asst. cameraperson				
stock footage									
finished animation									
editing & lab									

QUOTED PRICE INCLUDES ALL ITEMS ABOVE EXCEPT WHERE NOTED BELOW:

1. Written quotations rendered by (producer) become contracts only when signed by an authorized representative of your firm. Such contracts supersede any preliminary verbal estimates or quotations.

2. Quotations are only for work according to the original Film Production Specifications and Responsibility for Requirements. If through client error, omission, addition, or change of mind work in progress or work accomplished must be done a second time or more, all such extra work and overtimes will carry an additional charge at current rates for that work.

3. All contracts are made contingent upon wars, strikes, floods, accidents, or other contingencies beyond control of (producer), its assigns or representatives.

4. It is agreed that in the event of termination of work in progress covered by its quotation, that (producer) be reimbursed for all authorized expenditures, time charges, liabilities, and other outstanding contracts made in your behalf.

NET PRICE QUOTED: TERMS OF PAYMENT:

[   ]   [1/3]   [1/3]   [1/3] *

First shooting date:_____
Estimated time for delivery of answer print:_____
Estimated time for delivery of release prints:_____

For:_____
by:_____   by:_____
sig:_____   sig:_____
date:_____   date:_____

_____
*One-third at beginning of production; one-third at interlock; one-third at answer print.

General Provisions

1. This agreement and the net price set forth herein shall not be binding (on producer) until the agreement is countersigned by the client. This agreement shall supersede any preliminary verbal estimates, quotes, or other agreements relating to the subject matter.

2. Quotations are only for work according to the original Film Production Specifications and Responsibility for Requirements. If through client error, omission, addition, or change of mind, work in progress or work accomplished must be redone one or more times, all such extra work and overtimes will carry an additional charge at current rates for that work.

3. Upon completion of production of the film(s) and full payment thereof, all rights, title and interest in the film(s), and any component parts thereof shall vest in client.

4. Payment of the net price herein shall be made in the following manner:
   - one-third (1/3) upon commencement of production
   - one-third (1/3) upon interlock
   - one-third (1/3) upon delivery of an answer print.

5. The client will have the right to cancel this agreement by written notice to the producer at any time prior to completion of the film(s). In such event, the producer will be entitled to reimbursement of all direct costs and expenses which it has incurred in connection with the production of the film(s) to the date of cancellation, plus a sum equal to 35 percent of such direct costs and expenses. If the payments theretofore received by the producer shall exceed said sum, the producer will make the appropriate refund. If such payments were less than such sum, the client will make the appropriate additional payment.

6. In the event that the production of the film(s) hereunder shall be prevented due to act of God, strikes, or other contingencies beyond the control of the producer, the delivery date of the film(s) will be appropriately postponed.

7. The client will indemnify and hold harmless the Producer with respect to any and all damages, costs, judgment, penalties, including reasonable counsel fees, and all losses of any kind which may be obtained against, imposed upon, or suffered by the producer, by reason of the use of any products or material in the film(s) supplied by the client. Similarly, the producer will indemnify and hold the client harmless with respect to any such material supplied by the producer.

8. Upon completion of the production and payment to the producer, the producer will deliver to the client all prints and negatives of the film(s). If the client shall request the producer to retain negatives, the producer will secure all necessary fire and other loss insurance with respect to the storage of such negatives and the client will reimburse the producer the amount of the premium.

THE BIDDING PROCESS

Many film contracts are awarded only after the job goes out "to bid." In most of these cases, the film is already conceptualized and the production details are worked out. The job is normally contracted to the responsible producer who quotes the lowest price. Federal government agencies are required by law to award the contract to the lowest bidder. Many state and local government agencies also work this way. Private firms that use the bidding process often allow themselves a bit more leeway, considering the producer's talent and past experience as important criteria in the selection process, even when the proposed fee is higher than other bids.

If you contract to make a film through the bid process, be sure that the production details are understood by all concerned. Get the specifications in writing. It can be costly to you if things are not absolutely clear in the original agreement.

Bid Requirements

There are some typical requirements that the producer encounters when bidding on a film. Some of these are script meetings, the deadline date, bonding, revisions, releases, ownership of the film, payment, and film specifications.

- The due date for the completed film is reasonably firm; however, unexpected delays (that necessitate a later delivery date) can usually be negotiated between the producer and the client.

- The producer is typically required to provide the client with a bond that equals the contracted price, as a form of guarantee.

- If the producer suggests any revisions to the film, these must be approved by the client before the changes are made. The producer is responsible for extra expenses unless authorization is obtained in advance.

- It is up to the producer to obtain releases for talent, locations, music, and so on. The producer also pays any music royalties or television clearance fees.

- The client is entitled to ownership of all stock footage, sound tapes, or anything else resulting from the production. The producer may not copy any of the film without advance permission from the client.

- The producer will be required to make a film that is of good technical quality and answers the objectives of the client. The producer can be told to reshoot any work not deemed acceptable.

Presenting Your Response

When you submit a bid, express it in terms that pinpoint what you will and will not do for the money offered. Normally, a bid is submitted in the form of a letter restating the client's requirements and adding other conditions for production and delivery. The bid should refer to the client's request by name; it should quote your fee; it should describe the length of the film and the type of film stock; and it should specify whether you or the client are to supply the facility, equipment, and personnel.

You could be asked to offer a bid on a film that at that time does not have a script. This can be done if specifications are clear, with no gaps. If the limitations of the film have not been specified, costs may exceed the agreed-upon price. Express to the client that the price can vary depending on the logistics of a particular production.

- The communications objective is your bible.

- The story treatment is your promise.

- The distribution and promotion plan is your future.

- The budget breakdown is your connection with reality.

- Remember that the budget contains more costs than you wish to consider. Underbudgeting will cost you either money or goodwill.

- Promises do not pay bills; never begin production until the contract is signed.

PART THREE—PRODUCTION DATA

This section covers several types of forms commonly used as production records. There are two general areas to consider—personnel and logistics. It's likely that some of the samples contain more detail than you will find necessary, but they may help you develop your own documentation. Accurate records can help you control all aspects of the production, but don't let the paperwork get in the way of efficiency. Too many forms can bog you down, but too few can leave you dangerously vulnerable.

Required personnel employment documents, such as the Employee's Withholding Exemption Certificate, are available from U.S. federal government offices.

PERSONNEL FORMS

Model Release Form

A written release should be obtained from each person who is recognizable in a scene, whether or not they are hired to appear in the film. Legal model release forms are available and should be a requirement for every production. If any model is younger than 21, a parental signature must also be secured.

MODELING • PERFORMING

NARRATION • WRITTEN EXTRACT

RELEASE

SUBJECT_____
PRINT

PROJ. # _____
HRS. WORKED

For value received and without further consideration, I hereby consent that all photographs taken of me and/or recordings made of my voice and/or written extraction, in whole or in part, of such recordings or musical performance

at_____on_____19_____

by_____for (Company) may be used by (Company) and/or others with its consent, for the purposes of illustration, advertising, or publication in any manner.

SUBJECT_____
SIGNATURE

Street_____City_____State_____Zip_____

IF SUBJECT IS A MINOR UNDER LAWS OF STATE WHERE MODELING IS PERFORMED

GUARDIAN_____
SIGNATURE

GUARDIAN_____
PRINT

Street_____City_____State_____Zip_____

Date_____

Daily Time Card

The larger production houses generally have as many daily time card formats as they have unions. More often than not, each separate union requires different information to be filed. If you encounter such a situation, there are data processing service organizations available that will set up the elaborate punch-card systems required to effectively compile this information. With smaller, nonunion organizations you will probably find that one or two time cards at most will do.

DAILY TIME CARD

Name_____ Number_____

Date_____ Occupation_____

		Write in Time Below		Punch Clock Below
Time Started Work or Time of Call			In	
Time Finished Work			Out	
Picture or Job	Hrs.	First Meal Period	Out	
			In	
		Second Meal Period	Out	
			In	
		Third Meal Period	Out	
			In	

		PAYROLL USE ONLY	
		Hrs.	Amount
	Regular Overtime		
Approved	Double Time		
Dept. Head			
	TOTAL		

_____
Employee's Signature

Note: Unless otherwise authorized and noted a minimum of one hour will be deducted for Meal Periods.

LOCATION INFORMATION

Name of Location_____

Time

Traveling time—Studio to Location:

Traveling time—Location to Studio:

Check mode of Transportation:

Train ☐   Truck ☐   Auto/Bus ☐

Actor's and Model's Work Report

This form is used to develop a work profile for each actor or model from their daily time sheets. It should be filled in on a weekly basis and should include all times from makeup call to dismissal. An accumulated weekly total, as well as time and one-half and maximum time accumulations, should be calculated and shown on the form. The data collected on these forms will be very useful in controlling costs for your current production and can also be used in planning budget estimates for subsequent productions.

ACTOR'S AND MODEL'S WORK REPORT

Production Unit_____

Name_____ Part_____ Production No._____

Date	Make-Up Call	Set Call	Lunch Out	Lunch In	Dinner Out	Dinner In	Dismissed	Make-Up Time	Accum. 10 hr. Max.	Time and a Half	Over 10 hr. Max	Late Time Ded.	Total
Sun.													
Mon.													
Tues.													
Wed.													
Thur.													
Fri.													
Sat.													

Accumulative 40-hour week

Hours after 40—time and ½

Over 10 hours per day—not accum.

Total _____

Transportation—Lunch Sheet and Call Sheet

These forms are often used for large-scale productions, particularly for theatricals. They are normally posted on bulletin boards in the work area to inform the cast and crew of the latest production information. Some producers combine these two forms on one sheet when the production is not too complex.

TRANSPORTATION—LUNCH SHEET

Picture No.	Set No.	Date	Location	Rain or Shine Weather Permitting	
Requirements			Meals	Car	Bus	Leave Time

Requirements	Meals	Car	Bus	Leave Time
STAFF				
Producer				
Asst. Producer				
Secretary				
Director				
1st Asst. Director				
2nd Asst. Director				
Script Clerk				
Production Mgr.				
Asst. Production Mgr.				
Unit Mgr.				
Asst. Unit Mgr.				
Location Mgr.				
Extra Asst. Director				
Extra Script Clerk				
Dialogue Director				
Technical Advisor				
Musical Advisor				
ART DEPT.				
Art Director				
Asst. Art Director				
Sketch Artist				
CAMERA DEPT.				
1st Camera				
Operators				
Asst. Camera				
Stillman				
MAKE-UP DEPT.				
Co-Makeup Man				
Extra Makeup Man				
Body Makeup Woman				
Co-hairdresser				
Extra Hairdresser				
PLAYERS				
Cast				
Stand-ins				
Extras				
Minors				

Requirements	Meals	Car	Bus	Leave Time
CAMERA EFFECTS				
Process Camera				
Operators				
Asst. Camera				
PROPERTY DEPT.				
1st Prop				
2nd Prop				
Set Dresser				
ELECTRICAL DEPT.				
Gaffer				
Best Boy				
Still Electrician				
Wind Machine Oper.				
SOUND DEPT.				
Mixer				
Boom Operator				
Recorder				
Cableperson				
WARDROBE DEPT.				
Co-Wardrobe Man				
Co-Wardrobe Woman				
MINIATURE DEPT.				
Special Effects Person				
CASTING DEPT.				
Casting Director				
Asst. Casting Director				
GRIP DEPT.				
1st Grip				
2nd Grip				
Extra Grips				
CONSTRUCTION				
Carpenters				
Sign Painters				
Scenic Painters				
CUTTING DEPT.				
Cutters				
Asst. Cutters				
Projectionist				
PUBLICITY DEPT.				
Publicity Person				

MISCELLANEOUS					
Plumbers					
First Aid Nurse					
Studio Police					
Watchperson					
TRANSPORTATION DEPT.					
Bus Drivers					
Truck Drivers					
Car Drivers					

CALL SHEET

Producer_____Date_____

Production No._____Shooting Call_____

Title_____Director_____

Crew Report To_____

Crew Call_____

SETS
1.
2.
3.
4.
5.
6.

Cast	Character	Ward	Set
Doubles			
Extras			

CREW CALLS

Camera Oper.	
Asst. Camera Oper.	
Electrical Operators	
Grips	
Property Person	
Makeup Person	
Hairdressers	
Sound Mixer	
Boom Person	
Cable Person	
P.A. Operator	
Camera Effects	
Special Effects Person	
Painter	
Laborers	
Drivers	

LOGISTICAL FORMS

Script Breakdown

Most producers will design a Script Breakdown Form to suit their individual requirements. It is a good idea, however, to set this form up with the assistance of the camera technician because he or she will be very much involved in its use.

Any slating notes indicated should include tape reel numbers when shooting double-system lip synchronization. Minor revisions of the script along the way should also be noted.

SCRIPT BREAKDOWN

Production Title

Set	Sequence	Location

Period	Season	Day/Night	Total No. Script Pages

Cast	Bits	Scene Numbers and Synopsis
	Extras	

Process—Effects—Construction	

Music—Miscellaneous	

Props—Action; Props—Animals	

Assistant Director's Breakdown Sheet

During any large and complex production, an Assistant Director should be hired. A Breakdown Sheet will help the Assistant Director in organizing and planning the production as well as in avoiding wasted postproduction time. The Breakdown Sheets should be compiled in a binder and carefully numbered by scene and sequence.

ASSISTANT DIRECTOR'S BREAKDOWN SHEET

Sequence No.

Picture No._____ Set No._____ Sheet No._____

External_____

Internal_____

Scene

Costume No.

Scene Numbers	No.	Cast

Total Scenes | Total Dialogue | No. Pages | Day/ Night

Description

Props	Atmosphere	Bits

Cars—Livestock	Special Effects	Music

Camera and Accessory List

A detailed equipment list is a necessity particularly when you travel; it will provide information both for budgeting and insurance purposes. Keep enough copies of the completed form to protect against loss of the original. When crossing international borders, remember that customs will request an itemized list (with equipment serial numbers); you will pay duty on any equipment not listed with the customs office.

CAMERA AND ACCESSORY LIST

Date_____

Camera Operator_____Studio_____Location_____Job # _____

CAMERAS:
- ☐ BNC, REFL.
- ☐ BNC
- ☐ R35
- ☐ NC, REFL.
- ☐ NC
- ☐ STD., REFL.
- ☐ ARRI
- ☐ CP-16
- ☐ ECLAIR NPR/ACL

MOTORS:
- ☐ 110 V Variable
- ☐ 110 V Sync
- ☐ 220 V Sync
- ☐ High Speed
- ☐ Voltage Regulator, 110V or 220V with extra fuses
- ☐ Batteries
- ☐ Charger
- ☐ Extra cables
- ☐ Constant Speed Motor with extra fuses

MAGAZINES:
List quantity:
BNC, R35, NC 1000s_____STANDARD 1000s_____
R35 400s_____INVERTED OR REG.
STANDARD 400s_____
Other_____

ACCESSORIES:
- ☐ Sound Slate
- ☐ Changing Bag
- ☐ Camera Cover
- ☐ Rain Cover
- ☐ Wide Angle Matte Box Filter Adapter
- ☐ Camera Reports
- ☐ TV Ground Glass
- ☐ Variable Diffusion for_____
- ☐ Optical Glass
- ☐ Other_____
- ☐ Umbrella
- ☐ Tie Down Chains
- ☐ Tilt Wedge
- ☐ Heavy-Duty Geared Tilt Wedge
- ☐ Matte Cutter
- ☐ Periscope
- ☐ Bridge Plate
- ☐ Camera Tape
- ☐ Hot Plate
- ☐ Heated Barney

LENSES:

	BNC	NC	NPR	ACL	ARRI	CP-16
18 mm						
20 mm						
25 mm						
28 mm						
30 mm						
32 mm						
40 mm						
50 mm						
75 mm						
90 mm						
100 mm						
150 mm						

ZOOMS:
- [ ] 10 to 1
- [ ] 12 [ ] 15 [ ] 21 [ ] 23 [ ] 25
- [ ] 1X [ ] 2X

- [ ] 35 to 140 [ ] with proxars & following filters
- [ ] 12 [ ] 15 [ ] 21 [ ] 23 [ ] 25
- [ ] 1X [ ] 2X [ ] 85 [ ] 85B [ ] 85N3
- [ ] 85N6 [ ] Polarizing [ ] Other

FILTERS:
Circle: GELATIN 3 in. x 3 in.—12 15 21 23 25 56
23A/56 85 85B 85N3 85N6 .10ND .20ND .30ND .50ND
.60ND .70ND .90ND 1.00ND Other_____
Filters; Special series for following lens:
(specify filters in space):
18 mm_____ 90 mm_____
20 mm_____ 100 mm_____
25 mm_____ 150 mm_____
28 mm_____ Other_____
30 mm_____

HEADS: [ ] Geared [ ] Friction [ ] Fluid [ ] Other

TRIPODS:
- [ ] Hi Hat on Board   [ ] Hydraulic
- [ ] Standard (heavy-duty) [ ] Pro Jr. Standard
- [ ] ¾ (heavy-duty)   [ ] Pro. Jr. Baby
- [ ] Baby (heavy-duty)
- [ ] Other_____

FILM:* 1000'_____ 400'_____ 200'_____ 100'_____

SHIPPING:
- [ ] Empty Cans; Amt.____   [ ] Black Bags; Amt._____
- [ ] Shipping Tape   [ ] Shipping Cartons;
- [ ] Labels; Amt._____   Amt._____
- Other_____

DOLLIES:
- [ ] Crab w/extra Extensions [ ] Houston-Fearless
- [ ] Western   [ ] Other

---

*For information on the selection and use of *KODAK* and *EASTMAN* motion picture films, see the section entitled Kodak Resources, page 92.

Breakdown of Location Requirements

The Breakdown of Location Requirements List is similar to the equipment form; it represents a comprehensive inventory of cast and crew, properties, and miscellaneous items such as wardrobe, sets, and vehicles.

BREAKDOWN OF LOCATION REQUIREMENTS

Date_____

1st Unit_____ 2nd Unit_____

Prod. No._____ Title_____ Director_____

Set_____ Location_____ Leaving Date____

Scene Numbers_____ Black & White_____

Color_____

STAFF	CAST & WARDROBE #
Producer	
Director	
Unit Manager	
Asst. Director	
2nd Asst. Director	
Extra 2nd Asst. Dir.	
Art Director	
Dialogue Director	
Technical Director	
Script Clerk	
1st Camera Operator	
Camera Operator	
Ex. Asst. Camera Loader	
Camera Mechanic	
Technicolor Technician	
Still Camera Operator	
Mixer	
Boom Opr.	Total
Recorder	Miscellaneous Notes
Cable Person	
Radio Operator/P.A.	
Makeup Person	
Ex. Makeup Person	
Body Makeup Person	
Hairdresser	
Ex. Hairdresser	
Wardrobe Person	
Ex. Wardrobe Person	
Tailor/Seamstress	
Location Timekeeper/Checker	
Location Auditor	
Location Person	
Publicity Person	
_____Total	

BITS & EXTRAS	CREW
_____Bits	Property Person
_____Extras	Asst. Property Person
_____Stand-ins	Ex. Property Person
_____Doubles	Set Dresser
_____Minors	Grip
_____Stuntpeople	Asst. Grip
_____Singers	Painter
_____Dancers	Laborer
_____Musicians	Carpenter Foreman
_____Total	Carpenters
	Boom Oper. & Crew
	Gaffer
SPECIAL EFFECTS DEPT.	Best Boy
	Electricians
	Generator/Battery Person
	_____Total

SPECIAL EFFECTS DEPT.

SHOOT	Director
Keys	☐ Asst. Dir.
Glass Shot	
Straight	☐ Camera Operator
	☐ Script Clerk
	Operator
	Asst. Cam.
	Ex. Asst. Cam.
	Grips
	Electricians
	Prop. Person
	Effects Person
Total_____	

WARDROBE	MAKEUP & HAIRDRESSING

TRANSPORTATION	PROPS-SET DRESSING
Passenger Cars Staff Bus Extra Bus Camera Truck Sound Recording Truck Grip Truck Wardrobe Truck Electrical Truck Property Truck Generator Truck Boom Truck Construction Truck Mechanic _____Total	
	LOCAL HELP & EQUIPMENT
	_____Cars _____Buses _____Trucks _____Drivers _____Total
TECHNICAL/EFFECTS	**MEALS**
	Staff_____ Cast_____ Bits & Extras_____ Local Extras_____ Crew_____ Drivers_____ Spec. Effects_____ Misc._____ Local Help_____ _____Total

MISCELLANEOUS NOTES	
Batteries for wild shots Location permits Banking facilities Local union labor Child labor laws Time cards on crew Identification cards Ship film & reports Film crates & labels Insurance & taxes Train & plane schedules P.A. System Wind machines Electrical hookup Work lights	Weather reports Weather protection Special cleaning (costumes) First aid & Medical supplies Room & meals Dressing rooms Wardrobe space & racks Makeup room & tables Tables & benches Boom or dolly track Radio contact with studio Walkie-talkie Special camera mounts Rushes (projection room)

Daily Production Report

A Daily Production Report is essential to effective record keeping. It is used to record an overall running total for each day's events. The filled-in form will also provide planning information and status as well as progress on a production. You can readily see that a simpler form may be used for less complex productions. The comprehensive form shown here, however, is an administrative workhorse and can be applied to most productions.

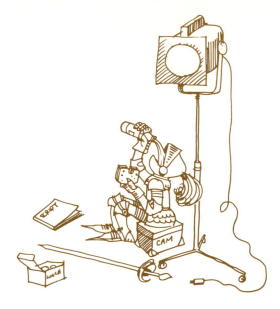

DAILY PRODUCTION REPORT

	No. Days Estimated		No. of Days on Picture			
Sound Stage Studio Lot Location			Rehearsals	Idle	Work	Total

Director_____ Date_____
Working Title_____ Date Started_____
Picture Number_____ Estimated Finish Date_____

Set_____
Set No._____ Location_____
Company Called_____ Time Started_____ Lunch: From_____ Till_____ Time Finished_____

SCRIPT SCENES AND PAGES	Script	Pages	MINUTES	SETUPS	ADDED SCENES	RETAKES	STILLS
Scenes in Script	_____	_____	Previous___	Previous___	Previous___	Previous___	Previous___
Taken Previous	_____	_____	Today___	Today___	Today___	Today___	Today___
Taken Today	_____	_____	Total___	Total___	Total___	Total___	Total___
Total to Date	_____	_____					
To be Taken	_____	_____					

Scene No.								
Credits								
Addit. Scenes								
Retakes								
Sound Tracks								

PICTURE NEGATIVE			MAGNETIC RECORDING MATERIALS		
GOOD	WASTE	DRAWN	GOOD	WASTE	DRAWN
Used Previous____	Previous____	Previous____	Used Previous____	Previous____	Previous____
Used Today____	Today____	Today____	Today____	Today____	Today____
Used to Date____	To Date____	To Date____	Used to Date____	To Date____	To Date____
Total Used to Date____ On Hand____			Total Used to Date____ On Hand____		

DAILY PRODUCTION REPORT

CAST—Contract & Day Players Worked-W; Rehearsal-R; Hold-H; Finished-F; Started-S; On call-C	W S R	H F C	Time Called	Time Dismissed	Hours Out for Meals	Cumulative Hours	Hrs. Week Complete	EXTRAS USED # Straight	Overtime
								MISCELLANEOUS on daily check	

ADVANCE SCHEDULE

Date_____Time Called_____Location_____

Set_____

Remarks_____

_____

Production Manager_____Assistant Director_____

- You can't keep track of all the work without accurate records.

- Forms are not creative; forms allow you to keep tabs on production so that you can continue to be creative.

- Look at it this way, would you trust a producer you didn't know? You can show the people who work for you that you care to protect their interests by requiring the paperwork necessary for you to remain in control of costs.

PART FOUR—POSTPRODUCTION

COORDINATING THE ACTIVITIES

The postproduction phase of filmmaking begins with the processing of your camera-original films and ends with the creation of client release prints for distribution. Postproduction is a mechanically complex process that will probably include all of the following and more:

- Camera-original film processing and workprinting—edge numbering, determining emulsion positions and winds, single- and double-perforated stocks, etc.
- Optical effects—wipes, titles, animation, etc.
- Picture editing—continuity, pacing, cutaways, flashbacks, etc.
- Soundtrack preparation—magnetic and optical tracks, transfers, music selection, sound effects, mixing, etc.
- Printing of A and B rolls and intermediates for production of release prints—16 mm or super 8, print quantities, price per foot, scene-to-scene color correction, etc.

At this point in the filmmaking process, you are giving up the close personal control you had during production. Now you have to rely on other people as well as the decisions you made during preproduction planning. You can remain in control of the business side of postproduction if you know, in detail, what is required and if you can get that message across to your service groups—film laboratories, sound recording studios, editing equipment rental houses, optical houses, animation studios, and so on.

Regardless of the service you request, and regardless of the group you work with, *get it in writing*. Face-to-face discussions and telephone calls are necessary for efficient workflow; but when it comes to specifying what you want, when you want it, and how much it will cost, a written document—usually in the form of a purchase order—is a must.

A detailed purchase order helps everybody. Before you write it, you should look beyond the particular service you need. Look at the project as a whole and judge how the service fits aesthetically, mechanically, and financially. Although you have the original camera footage and sound tapes in hand and feel you know all of the reasons for continuing with this part of the production, writing an *accurate* purchase order allows you another opportunity to review your *real* needs.

The purchase order will serve as a record of costs for budgetary reviews on the current production. It will also prove useful in computing your tax liabilities and in planning other projects.

From the supplier's point of view, the purchase order specifies the exact requirements for the job, which allows them to figure your costs more accurately and perhaps even give you a more favorable price.

If any questions or problems arise while the job is in progress, a purchase order will also serve as a common point of reference. In fact, to avoid potential problems, talk with your supplier *before* preparing the purchase order to determine any special requirements. You can even ask for suggestions on areas that could be cut back without compromising the quality of your film. Advice is free, and it may save you money.

Shown below is a listing of basic details that should be covered in your purchase order.

Company_____
Street_____
City_____State_____
Telephone_____
Job Number,_____
Job Description_____
Purchase Order Number_____
Date of Request_____
Description of Materials Being
   Supplied_____

Description of Services
  Desired_____
Delivery Date_____
Estimated Cost_____
Work Requested By_____
Deliver To_____

Note: All costs 10 percent or above the estimates must have prior written approval.

When dealing with any supplier, indicate that all charges exceeding the estimated price by 10 percent or more must have your prior written approval. You are then protected from unexpected costs that can drive a film over budget.

CHOOSING THE FILM LABORATORY

During postproduction, you will be spending quite a bit of time and money with a film laboratory of your choice, so locating the "right" lab is extremely important. Ideally, you should have some "feeling" for a lab early in the production phase, before you have 3000 feet of exposed film on your hands and are wondering what to do with it. How do you find that lab?

Generally, the lab that gets your business will be the one whose capabilities best match the requirements for your particular job. Every lab is different in terms of the technical services it offers, its attitude toward clients, its personnel, its track record on similar projects, its size and location, its price structure, and so on. You must weigh all of these factors against the job at hand to reach the proper match.

Of course, nearly every production has different requirements. A production filmed in 35 mm for television distribution will most likely go to a different lab than a job shot in 16 mm for reduction to super 8 and use as point-of-purchase advertising in local supermarkets. Your challenge as an efficient businessperson is to find the lab that can satisfy the greatest number of your needs on schedule and within budget. At best, you are faced with a number of trade-offs. For example, consider the question of big lab versus small lab.

The big lab usually offers more competitive pricing, more complete in-house capability, and excellent quality control. On the other hand, its bigness may result in your smaller job taking a back seat to "important" productions, in difficulty finding the person in charge of your job, and so forth.

The small lab, on the other hand, *usually* offers custom handling of your job and easy access to the right people for advice and counsel. The small lab *may* have to charge more to support their custom operation, *may* have to subcontract more of your job, and *may* not produce as high-quality an end product.

Look at the problem another way. Suppose you are a beginning filmmaker aspiring to professional status. Your camera-original and release print footage will probably be less than that produced by the well-established professional. Also, it will very likely be less demanding technically (optical effects, complicated sound mixes, etc.). It is even possible that you will need a bit more coaching than the long-time producer. Compromising a bit on the price to get the benefits a smaller lab could offer may be the right approach in this situation.

How about a lab's location? If you choose a lab that is significantly distant from your place of business (because it is well known or more price competitive), you will be faced with the potential hazards and increased costs of shipping valuable footage to and from the lab. Your daily communications with the lab will also be more difficult. Perhaps the smaller local lab would be a better choice in this case.

Obviously, the problem of choosing the right lab involves many variables and no pat answers. In the beginning, you will have to rely on information printed in comprehensive directories of motion picture services (see Part Seven), the advice of your peers (very subjective, at best), and your own intuition (does the place *feel* right?). As you become more experienced through comparative shopping and experimentation, the task of choosing your lab will become easier.

Once you have made your choice, get to know the personnel as well as possible and tell them as much as you can about yourself, your needs, and your style. The more they know about you and your production, the better they can service you.

Picture Editing

When you arrive at the editing phase of your production, you will need suitable editing equipment. If you own all the gear required, fine. If not, your film lab or local motion picture equipment rental house can help. Be careful, however, to tailor your equipment needs to the production schedule and budget. Highly sophisticated flat-bed editing facilities are a delight to use, but they are expensive to rent. With a small budget, you can keep your costs down by using a standard rewind table with synchronizer block.

Optical Effects

Optical effects such as wipes, dissolves, superimposed titles, split screens, and animation all add impact to your production. Bear in mind, however, that as your requirements for optical effects become more sophisticated, so does the price.

Simple effects such as fades and dissolves can be accomplished in the film lab during the printing process. More complex effects—split screen, freeze frames, mat work—require the services of an optical house. And when you consider the use of animation, the costs really begin to climb.

The basic message in this area is still to get all your requirements in writing. If you have done your preproduction homework, you will know what you want. If you communicate your needs concisely to the people doing your work, chances are good that you will stay within your budget.

Sound Tracks

You will undoubtedly have to create a supporting sound track for your film. To arrive at the finished track, your lab or cooperating sound recording studio will have to combine your location sound tapes with all the other sound inputs you have chosen—music, special sound effects, off-camera narration—into a professionally mixed optical sound track that is then printed onto your release prints along with the picture information.

One word of caution. Let the other professionals do their job. That is why they are in business. Your job is to tell them exactly what you want and then come to the mixing sessions well prepared. Plan the session before the actual recording date. Prepare accurate, easy-to-read logs. Organize and label your sound tapes to the very best of your ability. Since mixing is an expensive operation, good preplanning will pay off handsomely.

Production of the Finished Film

At this point, most of the final activity—answer print production/approval and printing of the release prints—again centers around the film laboratory. As before, know what you want and fully document those needs to the lab. After reviewing the first answer print, note all revisions that took place. Afterthoughts on subsequent answer prints may result in *payment* for more than one answer print. When those top-quality release prints are delivered, you will be well prepared to begin your next step—distribution.

- *"When the shooting was over, we thought we were home free."*
- *"We were going to save it in editing."*
- *"I don't know where the time went."*
- *"I'll never use that lab again."*
- *"I thought we'd save money by using some friends."*
- *"I didn't know it would cost so much."*
  —a former filmmaker

PART FIVE—
FILM DISTRIBUTION AND PROMOTION

Early involvement with a professional film distributor is essential in getting a general-interest film production to its target audience. Whether you are aiming at a large single audience or widely diversified audiences, a distribution service is an excellent vehicle for publicizing and communicating your film's message.

This part covers general considerations for distribution planning, the potential distribution channels for reaching mass audiences, important film ingredients influencing distribution methods, and the many services offered by the distributor (including promotional pieces, print inventory, supporting materials, film maintenance, etc).

GENERAL MARKET CONSIDERATIONS

"We have just made a new film. Could you come over and take a look at it and give us some suggestions for distribution?" This type of request (which originates from film producers or from the sponsors of a producer's film) is too often heard by professional film

distributors. Actually, the above question should be answered at the *planning* stage, *not* after the film is "in the can." Early in the game, consider not only *why* the film, but also *where* the film.

Unfortunately, film producers are often not well-equipped to communicate to their clients all of the effective distribution alternatives. If you feel at all uncomfortable with any of the distribution areas, get in touch with a film distributor who can answer your questions and handle your specific needs.

Not all industrial films are suitable for mass distribution, nor is their target a mass audience. Films are often produced to sell a client's product, point of view, or service to an extremely narrow market (e. g., medical films, military films). These films are carefully aimed at the target audience and usually delivered directly by the sponsor or his or her sales personnel. Professional distribution is normally not required for this type of film. This part is really addressed to the films that are made for unclassified or general audiences.

Nontheatrical films are generally directed to one or more of the six potential channels of distribution:

- Educational
- Special-interest groups
- Broadcast TV
- Cable TV
- Motion picture theatres
- Vacation resorts

Schools and special-interest groups account for the greatest utilization of sponsored films. Your films can also receive considerable visibility through the other four distribution channels. If you want to target your films at these areas most effectively, you should really contact a professional distributor.

Educational Category

There are four major subcategories in the educational field: grade school, junior high school, senior high school, and college. And, even within these there are many other subcategories, such as: boys, girls, and coeds.

Instructional films covering the following subject areas (among many others) are regularly shown to school-age students:

- Home Economics
- Science
- Physical Education
- Health
- Social Studies
- Business and Economics
- Vocational Guidance
- Arts and Crafts

Also within this age range are various nonschool youth organizations such as: Boy Scouts, Girl Scouts, Little League and other sports groups, YMCA, YWCA, etc.

Special-Interest Category

The special-interest grouping encompasses business and professional organizations, governmental organizations, religious groups, civic and social clubs, etc. Listed below are many of the areas that make up this large and diverse category:

- Business and Industry (e.g., oil companies, computer companies, electronics factories, automobile companies)

- Service and Fraternal Organizations (e.g., Rotary, Kiwanis, Masons)
- Church groups (e.g., Finance Committees, Pastor-Parish Relations)
- Sports groups—hunting, fishing, automobile clubs (NASCAR, SCCA), ski clubs, hiking clubs.
- Federal Government agencies (e.g., Internal Revenue Service, Health, Education, and Welfare Department)
- State Agencies (e.g., Department of Motor Vehicles, Transportation Department)
- Military branches (e.g., Army, Navy, Air Force, Marines)
- Hospitals

The above is not intended to limit the possibilities, but merely to point out the broad range of potential target audiences within the special-interest category.

Broadcast Television

Broadcast television (commercial and educational) provides the quickest method of exposing many thousands of viewers to your film at one time and at a surprisingly moderate cost. Your film should be original and aesthetically pleasing to be accepted for TV broadcast; it should also be appropriate for an audience of varying ages, educational backgrounds, and interests. A couple of points to remember are that running times of either 13½ or 27½ minutes are most suitable for the average TV station, and less prevalent film lengths include 3 to 5 minutes and 7 to 10 minutes for use as "fill" material (e.g., full-length film or sports event running less than a two-hour programming slot). Generally, TV stations broadcast from 2 to 4 hours of sponsored films every week.

Cable Television

Cable television (CATV) is a steadily growing market. Similar to broadcast TV, CATV enables you to show your film to many of the cable viewers (a total of about 10 million homes in 7000 communities) at a number of locations throughout the country. Again, your film should have wide audience appeal, be appropriate for many geographic areas, and run either 13½, 27½, 3 to 5, or 7 to 10 minutes. Although your film may be meant for a certain special-interest "regional" group, it could also be of interest to people in other communities.

Theatres

The public movie theatre is an effective means for showing your sponsored nontheatrical films; in this case, the most preferred running time ranges from 7 to 13 minutes. Sponsored films are often used in theatres to precede the "main attraction." Many different subjects are acceptable for showing to theatre audiences. Your film should basically entertain, exhibit professional picture and sound quality, and avoid glaring commercialism. Most theatres require 35 mm prints (blowups, of course, can be made from the 16 mm original).

Vacation Resorts

Vacation resorts are another excellent area for promoting your films. You have the opportunity to reach many community adult groups that do not normally meet in the summertime. Movies are frequently offered for evening entertainment by the management of resort hotels, motels, camps, or other similar vacation habitats. This approach enables you to communicate with a wide range of relatively affluent viewers (with the appropriate type of film, e.g., skiing, fishing, culture) in a leisurely and relaxed atmosphere.

IMPORTANT FILM INGREDIENTS

In addition to considering the categories of audiences and potential distribution channels, you should also examine some of the important parts of a successfully designed film: the running time, the advantages and disadvantages of using professional talent versus "industrial" talent, and the film content.

Running Time

The running time of your film will have a significant effect on the way it is distributed.

Generally, educators are looking for appropriate films running from 15 to 30 minutes. In fact, many will avoid the use of extremely short films simply because the time required to obtain and set up a movie projector cannot be justified for a few minutes of screen time.

Adult organizations, on the other hand, will normally shy away from films this long, preferring presentations that run less than 15 minutes.

Therefore, you should carefully evaluate the length of your film based on the target audience. You might even want to produce two different lengths (different versions) of the film to maximize usage for both the adult and the school audiences.

Professional Talent Versus "Industrial" Talent

One of your responsibilities is to decide whether to use recognized ("name") talent or unrecognized talent. There are advantages to using either type of talent (cost considerations and film impact).

The use of good industrial performers in place of "name" talent can result in an excellent film; for the most part, viewers are primarily concerned with the film's message.

If you decide to go with recognized talent, consider these potential (yet remote) conditions. An actor involved in your production could possibly do a film for a competitive company and create credibility problems. Or, such a personality might not be available when needed, could be too expensive, lose popularity, pass away, or even date a film.

On the other hand, there are certain films that require appropriate "stars" (e.g., films pertaining to major sports such as skiing, bowling, auto racing, soccer, football, baseball).

Film Content

Film content must be a blend of what the client deems important to get across to the public and the producer's interpretation of those aims. Some producers, unfortunately, make elaborate films strictly to win filmmaking awards and to gain recognition; the content and the cinematic techniques applied may be accentuated to that end. It is conceivable, therefore, that the client's/sponsor's original purpose for the film has been somewhat misdirected. The real objective is to meet all of your client's expectations.

DISTRIBUTOR SERVICES

The actual elements of film distribution are simple in theory but vastly more complex in practice. You might think that to successfully market your film you need only an audience and a method of getting the film to the viewers. However, distribution is really a more complex "science."

Mass audiences such as classroom students (kindergarten to college level) are fairly easy to locate. Other target audiences (skiers belonging to ski clubs and members of hunting and fishing "Rod and Gun" clubs, etc) are not particularly hard to reach because they belong to well-known organizations. However, certain desired target audiences are difficult to find and perhaps not as easily influenced toward using your film.

In this regard, women's clubs tend to be a difficult category. Many women's groups are organized for a specific purpose, and may not want to look at a wide range of films or even films directed to their immediate concern. Most are not as well established as comparable men's organizations, nor do they generally own 16 mm motion picture projectors. Very often, they do not even know how to obtain and/or operate the projector.

This section, then, covers the advantages of using film distributors and the techniques they use to help you and your sponsor determine less obvious target audiences.

Promotional Ideas

Efficient promotion can heavily affect overall film distribution. To assist the sponsor, supplemental "promo" literature (ranging from a single handout to a series of brochures and catalogs) can be prepared by the distributor. Regardless of the format chosen and the cost of producing such a promotional "unit," there will be an extra expense in getting materials to the audiences.

Obviously, a direct-mail system will play a vital role in getting promotional media to the film users; to help you, distributors have the latest comprehensive mailing lists of nationwide business and educational institutions.

The handling of promotional materials can range from self-mailers to elaborate catalogs. Costs for an outside vendor's services (layout and printing) are only part of the expenses that must be factored in; you may also be charged for mailing lists, handling, and of course postage.

Self-promotion by a sponsor who has a single film would cost more than any other "unit" listing several films for which promotional expenses could be amortized. The only time a distributor might charge the sponsor a special fee would be for a very unique promotion. If the sponsor's film is listed in general catalogs indicating numerous film availabilities, then there will not be a separate distributor's charge.

Print Inventory

Print inventory is virtually the key element in effective film distribution. The sponsor will need a sufficient number of prints on hand to adequately supply all of the intended target audiences. Unfortunately, many films are produced without consideration given to this subject. Frequently only a minimal budget is set aside for film printing costs.

If you think about the number of 16 mm movie projectors that are owned by business and industry, government, education, and other potentially interested organizations, there is practically no limit to print quantities that could be circulated for mass distribution.

Based on an old "rule of thumb" of

approximately 20 different audience bookings per print per year, a sponsor can roughly calculate how many audiences can be reached in a year on varying print inventories and thus estimate the cost of such distribution including prints and commercial circulation.

For instance, if you have 100 prints and approximately $9,500, you could potentially net up to a combination of 2,000 educational and special-interest audience bookings on a yearly basis. There would be an increase of roughly 25¢ per booking to reflect *only* the adult audience (without any school-audience shipments). Furthermore, if you distributed 40 broadcast TV prints, you could anticipate averaging 350 to 400 billable bookings with approximately 400 to 450 telecasts a year. Since cable TV is included here, the costs would average below total commercial television dollars. Based on current prices of $27.50 per booking for standard broadcast and $17.50 per booking for CATV, there would be about 200 standard broadcast billables at a cost of $5,500, plus 150 CATV billables at $2,600 for a total of $8,100.

Again, be sure you account for anticipated distribution costs in your planning and budgeting activities. Check with several film distributors concerning pricing for print inventory services and factor those expenses into the distribution plan. It would be unfortunate for you to discover late in the game that sufficient dollars were not set aside for proper film distribution.

Film sponsors like to get feedback—information on the usage of their prints. An "audience report card" is usually prepared by the distributor indicating: dates and times that the film was shown, the number of audience participants, etc. This data is generally tabulated into monthly and yearly reports which are sent to the sponsor.

Supporting Materials

Besides considering print inventory and distribution costs, you should also think about the possible use of printed "instructor or program chairperson" materials, as well as student or group member take-home pieces. Far too many films are sent to audiences without adequate support information; by merely supplying a business leader's (or teacher's) booklet or guide with the film, you can make it a much more appealing and meaningful package from the audience's standpoint.

Typical subjects include: a capsule description of the film, an in-depth discussion of the film's historical context, a precise presentation on the products involved (including prices), etc.

Other possible uses: hints on product features and usage, suggestions for discussion after the screening, demonstration kits for teachers, tidal charts for fishermen, game laws for hunters, or exercise suggestions for athletes.

Film Maintenance

Finally, most film distributors will offer a print maintenance program. Under such an agreement, your prints will be completely inspected for torn or open splices, torn sprockets or other imperfections, scratches, and missing footage. Early correction of these problems will protect your prints from possible damage and loss.

The distributor will place protective, colored head and tail leaders (complete with the address of the distributor) on the release prints, because:
- You can easily identify the film by title and print number.
- Color coding of the leader will immediately indicate if the print is heads or tails out (to determine if rewinding is necessary).
- The leader will indirectly guard against film loss through the mail, in the event that the film and its case become separated.
- The leader will protect the film from damages occurring by way of improper projector threading.
- The leader will clear the projector gate of dust and debris before the film is projected.

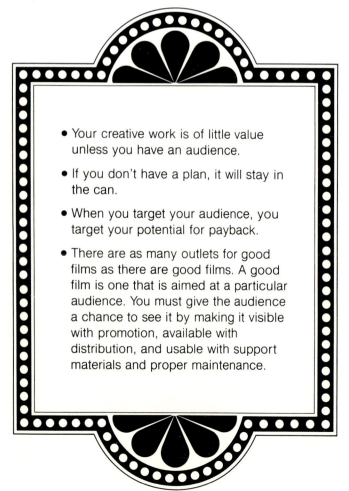

- Your creative work is of little value unless you have an audience.

- If you don't have a plan, it will stay in the can.

- When you target your audience, you target your potential for payback.

- There are as many outlets for good films as there are good films. A good film is one that is aimed at a particular audience. You must give the audience a chance to see it by making it visible with promotion, available with distribution, and usable with support materials and proper maintenance.

PART SIX—
DAILY BUSINESS ACTIVITIES

The business of filmmaking involves certain functions and responsibilities that do not fit naturally under the previous sections. Gathered here are topics covering forms of business, insurance regulations, the selection of a location for your filmmaking business, efficient management of finances, depreciation of equipment, warning symptoms of financial trouble, and a checklist for starting your own business. You may not need all of the information supplied in this part; take from it only what you want to use.

THE STRUCTURE OF YOUR BUSINESS

There are three principal forms of business organization:
- Sole proprietorship
- General partnership
- Corporation

Each form is quite different from the others, and one may be more suitable to your needs than another. For example, forming a partnership or corporation may be a better approach to generating capital funds than borrowing. Under either form, however, losses as well as profits will be shared with others.

The following paragraphs briefly discuss the advantages and disadvantages of three popular business structures. However, to avoid future complications and possible litigation, you should secure the services of a lawyer for advice on the type of organization that best fits your needs. Indeed, a lawyer who is versed in all aspects of business law will be a decided asset.

Sole Proprietorship

The advantages of this type of business are obvious. You are your own boss. You can come and go as you please. You share your profits with no one. However, these advantages are not gained without some sacrifice and compromise. You may find, unfortunately, that one person does not possess all the abilities required for a successful business. A person with limited assets cannot depend upon finding willing lenders if additional funds are needed. If your business fails, your home, your car, and other personal property may be subject to claim in addition to business assets.

The General Partnership

A partnership is generally defined as a voluntary association of two or more persons (co-owners) for the operation of a profitable business. It permits the pooling of the various abilities and capital of each partner. Agreement must be reached on how profits are to be divided. You should have a lawyer prepare partnership contracts that clearly define each partner's rights and duties.

When beginning your career, you might want to offset your lack of business knowledge by taking a partner who has experience. However, this means that you share authority and must accept some restrictions on your independence. You should exercise great care in choosing a partner because the personality and character of partners as well as their ability to render technical or financial assistance can affect the success of the business.

It is important to remember that the partnership means a responsibility for all of the obligations of the business on each partner individually. Debts incurred in the business or contracts made by any partner create a personal liability for all concerned. If a partner dies or withdraws from the business, the partnership is dissolved unless the original partnership agreement made provisions for the transition.

The Corporation

This form of business is rather uncommon in the filmmaking profession.

However, do not avoid this type of business arrangement merely because corporation and bigness seem to go hand in hand; they do not always. There are two main advantages to incorporating your business: (1) A corporation has the capacity for perpetual existence. It is not limited to your lifetime or those of your partners; (2) The owners (stockholders) are immune from personal liability. They can lose no more of their personal assets than those invested in the corporation. Note, however, that the major stockholder of a corporation having limited resources may be asked to personally guarantee the repayment of a loan.

The corporation, like other forms of organization, also has certain disadvantages: (1) Taxes are usually higher for the corporation than for sole proprietorship or partnership. (2) Since the corporation is a separate entity subject to specific state and federal laws, it requires more extensive record keeping and reporting. (3) Corporations are formed under specific laws for clearly defined purposes. To broaden the geographic area of operation or to change the range of activities, a corporation will usually be required to seek governmental approval of the changes.

Licenses, Taxes, and Government Regulation

If this is your initial experience in business, you must acquaint yourself with the permits, licenses, taxes, and hiring laws that apply to your filmmaking business. Local, state, and federal units of government will require that you obtain documents and submit reports on a broad range of business activities. Here are a few examples: employer identification number, seller's permit, sales tax bond, and registration with various tax and employee insurance agencies.

You may find yourself dealing with local zoning boards, local and state tax agencies, the state employment department, the state corporation commission, and various federal agencies such as the Internal Revenue Service, the Equal Employment Opportunity Commission, and the Occupational Safety and Health Administration. As indicated earlier, developing a close relationship with an attorney (who has had experience in dealing with all types of business affairs) will be advantageous in helping you over business hurdles and giving you more restful nights.

You may also find yourself responsible for collecting and accounting for sales taxes and for various employee tax withholding or insurance obligations. Some businesses have a separate bank account into which they deposit the tax funds. Your accountant can help in setting up a procedure for recording, reporting, and disbursing these funds.

Under the United States Tax Reform Act of 1976, individuals choosing to incorporate have certain advantages. Check with your accountant on these items: limited liability, transfer of ownership, hospitalization/health insurance programs that are tax deductible, the medical reimbursement plan (MRP), and retirement.

Insuring Your Business Against Measurable Risks

For ongoing business success, identify all possible risks and cover those that are important and insurable by purchasing the necessary insurance policies. Many profitable firms have gone out of business when hit by disaster (e.g., fire, flooding) because of inadequate insurance coverage. You should consider the following risk areas carefully and, working in cooperation with a reputable local insurance person, put into effect an insurance plan that will protect your assets and earning power from serious loss.

Liability to others: Responsibility to the public for incidents involving your production equipment, vehicles, etc, as well as responsibilities to your employees under workmen's compensation statutes.

Loss or damage of assets: Destruction by fire, explosion, windstorm, vandalism, riot, burglary, and other hazards; automobile collision, fire, and theft. In the case of a partnership, it may be advisable, in addition, to buy insurance on the lives of the partners. This makes possible the liquidation of a deceased partner's interest at a fair valuation and enables the surviving partner(s) to continue the business. In the absence of funds available from insurance proceeds, the surviving partner(s) may be forced to liquidate the business at a substantial loss. Similar coverage is available for the closely held corporation.

The importance of adequate insurance coverage cannot be overstressed; however, you should guard against buying unnecessary amounts of insurance or unneeded types of insurance. Generally, you should buy insurance against hazards that could cause serious loss and avoid trading dollars with insurance companies on lesser hazards that produce losses you are capable of absorbing as an operating expense. Do consider deductibles as a cost reduction device. Packaged insurance also tends to promote cost reductions while providing broader coverage. Discuss such points with your local insurance person and be sure he or she understands your needs.

One reminder—do not think of insurance as a substitute for good equipment maintenance. Avoiding a loss is infinitely preferable to having one, even when a well-designed insurance program is in force.

LOCATING YOUR BUSINESS

The location or relocation of your business may be one of the most important decisions you have to make. Location affects almost every facet of your business operations—clients, production costs, promotional efforts, employee satisfaction, and perhaps even the quality of your work. Never stop considering the possibility of relocating.

The choice of a good location can be narrowed down in the following manner: (1) select the town or city, (2) then select the area within the town or city, and (3) finally, select a specific site in the chosen area.

Selecting the city. The fact that you have lived in, or like, a particular community does not automatically make it an ideal site for locating your business. Some cities are growing while others are stable or even experiencing a decline. Growth in population, wealth, and business activity will be attractive to you as a prospective businessperson.

You should investigate the population trends, business concentrations, and other demographic information to decide the potential for adequate sales volume and profitable operation.

The number of other producers working in the area should also influence your choice of location. Even if there are several producers in the area, you may find that you can offer a better type of specific service to meet the needs of local firms. This decision should depend on thorough research into these needs and an honest assessment of one's own abilities to fulfill them.

The amount and character of industry in a given city are of great importance. In contrast to a city with diversified industries, a one-industry town is often vulnerable to seasonal and cyclical fluctuations. A strike could mean a temporary cessation of business. Look, also, for necessary suppliers of essential services.

Besides considering the present population and sources of filmmaking business already available, you should consider the probable future of the city or town. Is it likely to change from a major agricultural town to an industrial city? If it is industrial, how old and well established is it? How aggressive are the business leaders and civic associations?

Rent is a significant expense in the operation of most businesses; therefore, you should determine the average rental charges in the town you are considering. However, never choose a town solely on the basis of rent.

Most information about a location can be obtained from published data in libraries and from major suppliers, the Chamber of Commerce, state development agencies, and the research bureaus of various universities.

Personal considerations. In locating a small business, personal factors are more important than they are for a large business. Some of these are:

- A desire to locate among friends and acquaintances.
- A personal preference for a particular part of the country.
- A need to locate in a particular climate for reasons of health.

Choice of the hometown for personal reasons does not mean that it is an illogical decision. Credit is easier to obtain if you are already known. Your knowledge of the people and businesses, their habits, their likes and dislikes, and other local characteristics may be an asset that a stranger would pick up with difficulty. Friends and acquaintances could be your first clients and may give your business word-of-mouth publicity. However, it is usually a mistake to base patronage on friendship alone, and more of a mistake to expect it to be profitable.

Selecting the area. The next step is to decide in what part of the town to locate. If the town is small, there will be little choice. In larger cities, the volume of your business should determine the area to be chosen. The original investment may be so large that it is impossible to obtain sufficient sales to pay the high rent of a downtown spot. It is then necessary to select a suburban or industrial area of the city.

Selecting a site. Choice of the actual site within an area may be limited. Not very many buildings in a locality will be suitable and at the same time available for your use. You should check the traffic flow, parking facilities, street location, physical aspects of the building including type of lease, history of the site, and the amount, speed, cost, and quality of transportation.

Some locations appear to carry a jinx, and the businesses that occupy such sites seem doomed to failure. There are usually rational explanations for such failures, but you should know the history of the site before narrowing your choice.

Here is a good check sheet to use in evaluating sites. It is adapted from the Small Business Administration Management Aid No. 201, 1977.

Rating Sheet on Sites

Grade each factor: "1" for excellent, "2" for good, "3" for fair, and "4" for poor.

Factor	Grade
1. Centrally located to reach my market	_____
2. Materials and supplies readily available	_____
3. Quantity of available labor	_____
4. Transportation availability and rates	_____
5. Labor rates of pay/estimated productivity	_____
6. Local business climate	_____
7. Tax burden	_____
8. Quality of police and fire protection	_____
9. Housing availability for workers and management	_____
10. Environmental factors (schools, cultural and community atmosphere)	_____
11. Estimate of quality of site in 10 years	_____
12. Estimate of this site in relation to my competitors	_____
Total	_____

MANAGING YOUR FINANCES

When looking at any business you must remember that appearances can be deceiving. A business may appear to be established yet actually be going downhill, perhaps to the point of losing money. Although a business may be growing in sales volume, it may be lagging in profitability, especially when related to the growth of the economy and the decline in the purchasing power of the dollar. Only through use of adequate records can the financial health of your filmmaking business be assessed realistically. And only with reliable figures in hand will you have a sound basis for business decisions.

You should give careful consideration

to two kinds of capital funding: short-term or working capital and long-term or equity capital. Undercapitalization in either area can be serious. Short-term funds are those monies which will be necessary to satisfy cash flow requirements during the year. Long-term capital is used to satisfy such fixed asset requirements of the business as building purchase or renovation and equipment purchase.

It is usually best to begin the business with sufficient capital from your own personal resources or savings. In most cases, however, this is not a realistic possibility and other sources of funds must be considered. Those sources include family, friends, and business partners, as well as banks and other lending institutions. With any of these sources there will be a cost to your business. The cost includes interest charges, loss of full control, or both. Specific sources for financial advice include your local bank, the Small Business Administration, and small business investment companies.

Financial Records

You may feel that if you have sufficient records to meet the requirements for income tax returns, you have satisfied the accounting needs of your business. Unfortunately, there is much more to effective accounting control than simply being able to respond accurately to the Internal Revenue Service. In addition to end-of-the-year tax data, you must continuously monitor your business activities through an accounting system that is simple and understandable.

Basic accounting systems are not difficult to set up. Here are two ways: (1) If you have some accounting or bookkeeping training, keep the records, or (2) you can hire an accountant to initiate a proper accounting system and maintain the records thereafter yourself.

If you do seek outside help in maintaining your records, you have not relieved yourself of responsibility in the compilation of the data. You should be familiar with some basic accounting methods in order to evaluate and properly use the information that you

receive, and perhaps to suggest additional information that would be helpful. If you have not familiarized yourself with some basic accounting concepts, you may find your accountant is keeping your records in a manner convenient for him or her but not necessarily for you.

In addition to recording information that meets the requirements of government tax and payroll reporting, you should have records that assist you in making day-by-day management decisions. These records should be simple, understandable, timely, and inexpensive to maintain. Your own system should provide for methods of collecting, summarizing, reporting, and analyzing data. For collecting original data, use a book of original entry, commonly known as a journal. A ledger (book of accounts) should also be maintained for summarizing or classifying data. In the ledger, you should gather similar items together under the proper headings: cash, salaries, rent, depreciation of equipment, insurance, supplies, etc. Good accounting records should keep you adequately informed about:

- The kinds and values of assets owned.
- All debts owed by the business, including payroll and withholding deductions.
- Amounts owed to the business.
- Cash movements (bank balance, receipts, payments).
- Sales.
- Expenses classified by type of expenditure (also, expenses that are not current cash outlays such as depreciation of equipment and bad debts).
- Profits and losses (this information should be readily available, not just produced at the end of the year).

In today's world of automated business records, you should give some thought to the use of local and national computer services to assist you in the financial management of your business. Your accountant will know of the availability of such specialized service companies. In the future, the smaller firm will make more use of data processing services. A

real value in doing automated accounting is that you can gain comparative monthly analyses derived from thousands of small businesses like your own.

Although banking services have become very sophisticated in recent years, the standard checking account is still one of the simplest tools for keeping track of cash flow. You can account for payments and receipts by depositing all money coming in and writing checks for all money going out. Checks can prove extremely useful if the Internal Revenue Service calls for substantiation of some expenditure.

Pay small amounts under five dollars out of a petty cash fund. To keep track of such payments, make a log or fill out a simple petty cash voucher. This practice will provide information charging the expense to the correct account. When the petty cash fund is depleted, write a check to replenish it and record the charges against the appropriate accounts.

Credit purchasing is often more convenient than paying cash. Your credit rating is so important that you should protect it by paying all bills on time. You can make sure that you do not miss payments by keeping a bill file with a section for each day of the month. File the bills under the due dates as they come in and be sure to check if early payment could mean a cash discount. Pull the bills that are due (in advance) and avoid late payment penalties.

Note: You may not have the need, inclination, or temperament to get into higher levels of accounting methods; but for those of you who have the interest, read on.

Costs and Depreciation of Equipment

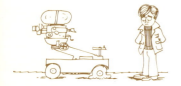

Keep careful records on all equipment whether it is owned or rented. These records should include equipment cost, cash payment if purchased on credit, monthly payments, remaining balance due, and the depreciated value. Keep an equipment record sheet and enter each payment as it is made. At the end of each year, calculate depreciation on

equipment and enter it on the equipment record. Keep in mind that depreciation is computed solely to express the cost of using your equipment. This figure represents a cost of doing business just as much as rent or utilities expenses.

There are two basic depreciation methods. The straight-line method charges off the same number of dollars for each year of the estimated useful life of an asset. It is easy to understand and requires a minimum amount of computation. Accelerated methods, such as the sum-of-the-years' digits (SOYD), double-declining balance, and units-of-production methods, charge a larger fraction of the cost of using an asset as an expense in the earlier years than in the later years. This approach is based on the fact that many assets are more valuable when relatively new; as they age, their mechanical efficiency (cameras, tape recorders) tends to decline, maintenance costs tend to increase, and as time passes there is an extremely good chance that better equipment will become available and make them obsolete.

The choice of the depreciation method is governed principally by tax considerations. An accelerated method will probably minimize taxes, although increases in income or in tax rates will work in the direction of reducing or eliminating the tax advantage. Once you have filed a tax return, you may find it difficult to change depreciation methods. Evaluate your own situation carefully with advice from your accountant or tax adviser, before choosing. Refer to Internal Revenue Service Publication 334, *Tax Guide for Small Business,* for depreciation methods and computations.

The Balance Sheet and Profit-and-Loss Statement

If your records are complete and accurate, you have the information necessary to compile the two basic financial reports used in successful business management—the balance sheet and the profit-and-loss statement. You should prepare these reports even if you are the only one who sees them.

Poor financial records can be a major cause of business failures, although poor records are not in themselves the cause of difficulty. But if they are inadequate, they leave you without a compass. You are unable to see the direction in which you are going. The first indication that something is really wrong may come too late.

The balance sheet shows the condition of the business on the closing date of the records. You can see how much cash you have, how much inventory is on hand, how much money clients owe your firm, how much is owed to creditors, and your equity (the money value of your interest in the business in excess of all claims against it). As a film producer, you should work continuously toward increasing the size of this net worth if your business is to grow. The balance sheet is so named because the total assets balance with the total liabilities and your own equity. It shows that everything owned by a business is financed either through ownership or borrowed funds.

The profit-and-loss statement is the summary of operations for a given period of time, usually between two balance sheet dates. It reflects operations by relating income received during the period to expenses necessary to generate sales. The net result is a profit (or loss), which is available to the producer to retain in the business (net worth increase) or to withdraw for personal use. These statements are most useful if they are prepared monthly or quarterly rather than annually.

Cost Control

One of the major financial stumbling blocks encountered by many film producers is that they fail to identify all of the real costs and maintain accurate records of them. When all costs are not included and deducted from total revenue, the producer falsely believes he or she is operating more profitably than really is the case. This is a dangerous situation for any business. It is imperative that records be kept accurately and analyzed frequently to identify any unfavorable cost trends.

Your control of costs will be made much easier if you start with a clear understanding of some basic classifications of costs. Bear in mind that a particular cost may be classified in more than one grouping, depending on the purpose for which the information is being collected.

There should be no difficulty in identifying real costs. Some clear-cut examples include payments made for utility services, employee wages, interest on loans, and rent. Implicit costs are not so easily identified. Implicit costs are those that would be charged for services if you secured these services from someone else. They include interest on capital you have invested in the business, rent for premises you own that are being used for business purposes, and a payment for your own services.

Another useful distinction is that between fixed and variable costs. Fixed costs are those that cannot be changed appreciably over the short term. Examples of fixed costs include base utility rates, license fees, and rent. Variable costs vary with the amount of production. As you increase your production, your variable costs will increase proportionately, and vice versa. Examples of variable costs include film, sound recording tape, and other supplies.

Operating Ratios

Another accounting technique that you can use to help measure and control your business activities is the operating ratio. A ratio indicates a relationship between two factors, such as sales and rent, sales and distribution expenditures, and so on. Figuring your operating ratios at the end of the year will help you find out whether you have made as much profit as you should have, and whether you have operated efficiently. You may discover that you are losing business by not spending enough on certain items. For example, a low distribution-sales ratio may mean that one of the causes of low profits is insufficient film distribution.

You can calculate certain ratios from your financial statements that will assist you in your managerial decision-making and in planning for future film productions. They can tell you what financial pressures and strains are affecting your business. Here are a few of the ratios that businesspeople commonly use:

Current Ratio: Divide current assets by current liabilities. The result shows how ready your business is to meet its current debt. Generally, a 2:1 ratio is safe.

Profit-On-Sales Ratio: Divide net profit by sales. This ratio demonstrates what part of each sales dollar is profit. The higher this ratio, the more efficiently your business is running.

Worth-To-Debt Ratio: Divide net worth by total debt. This ratio shows how your investment as producer and manager of the business compares with the total amount due to creditors.

Profit-To-Net-Worth Ratio: Divide net profit by net worth. An important ratio, this shows the producer's return on investments.

Sales-To-Working-Capital Ratio: Divide sales by working capital. This ratio tells how many dollars of sales the business makes for every dollar of working capital.

Average ratios and operating percentages are published periodically for many types of businesses by Dun & Bradstreet, Robert Morris Associates, and by some banks.

WARNING SYMPTOMS OF FINANCIAL TROUBLE

The information presented here is intended to help you to improve the financial performance of your filmmaking business. Admittedly, everyone will not be able to use these methods with equal success. Your job as a producer-manager requires you to recognize a trouble spot, to find out why it occurred, and to take corrective action immediately.

It is impossible to identify specifically all the problems you may encounter; however, there are several general symptoms that should warn you when trouble is brewing. Reduction of working capital, declining sales, a decrease of profits, and debt ratios that decrease each month are signals of definite problems. Unless you take corrective action, failure may be unavoidable.

Working capital provides the funds necessary for day-to-day operation of the business. It includes those assets of a business that change frequently from cash, to cost of operation, and to cash again. There should be enough capital to allow you to conduct your business without financial difficulty and to meet emergencies and losses without fear of failure. Adequate working capital (1) makes it possible to pay all maturing bills promptly and to take advantage of cash discounts, (2) ensures the maintenance of your credit standing, and (3) enables the business to operate more efficiently, e.g., with adequate capital, there are no delays in getting materials, services, and supplies due to credit difficulties.

A technique that can be employed to measure the adequacy of your working capital is the current ratio. A current ratio of 2:1 (assets to liabilities) is usually adequate. You and your accountant can determine the best relationship for your business and then attempt to maintain it. If the current ratio indicates a declining trend in your working capital, you should seek additional funds, tighten credit policy, leave more money in the business, and postpone further investments in equipment or other fixed assets.

Reductions in sales quickly lead to operating losses if allowed to continue. The methods needed to reverse a declining trend differ with the circumstances. You may wish to increase advertising expenditures to reach more target clients. Consider if a new service might increase profits. This is the time to cultivate new business by calling personally on more prospective clients.

CAUSES OF BUSINESS FAILURE

If your business should fail, you may lose your life's savings. Moreover, if you fail, you will suffer a real blow to your self-esteem. A small percentage of business failures are caused by physical disasters that could have been avoided by carrying adequate insurance. Most failures, however, can be attributed to the four factors dealt with in the following paragraphs.

Misjudgment of Client Needs: In some cases, the film producer who has failed will attribute the failure to heavy competition. Close analysis frequently indicates that this explanation is not adequate. Businesses succeed because they find and fill a need felt by a significant number of clients. Businesses fail because they make inaccurate or incomplete judgments about what clients need. As a professional filmmaker you have an individual and very personal service to offer. The challenge is to express your talent, your competence, and your availability in a way and at a time that will encourage clients to respond to you.

Lack of Capital: Starting a filmmaking business on a shoestring often leads to failure. Although adequate capital may have been provided, its *misuse* can result in an inability to meet obligations. Failure to pay maturing debts can force into insolvency an otherwise profitable enterprise.

Poor Location: Although a good location may deteriorate with the passage of time, such an occurrence is not likely in the short run. Most failures caused by bad location can be attributed to an exercise of poor judgment in the original selection of the location.

Premature Expansion: An unwise expansion of operations can be fatal. Expansion of any business should be financed soundly, preferably from earnings or equity capital contributions if such expansion is warranted. This calls for careful advance planning based on past business experience and an accurate measurement of the market. Never expand for subjective reasons such as prestige or convenience.

You have probably noticed a common factor in these four causes of business failure—*bad management.* Among the many interrelated causes of business failure, perhaps the most important basic cause is lack of skill in management. *You should never try to operate your own business unless you are confident that your management skills are at least as good as your skills in producing films.*

It's wise to continually work at improving your management efficiency. By applying many of the techniques mentioned in this book, you can avoid the possible disaster of business failure. Survey your own strengths and weaknesses. Learn more about the filmmaking business, marketing, and finance. You are the one who will reap the rewards of success—or suffer the bitter fruits of failure.

MANAGEMENT ASSISTANCE

The United States Small Business Administration (SBA) offers management assistance programs; the major goal is to promote the establishment, growth and success of small businesses. The need for this service is evidenced by failures that occur in the small business community every year.

The SBA estimates that managerial deficiencies cause nine out of ten business failures, and that many of these business failures could have been avoided had the owners received management assistance. Through the facilities of the Office of Management Assistance, the SBA works to improve the management capabilities of small businessmen and women.

In addition to Management Assistance officers who staff the counseling program, SBA draws from SCORE (Service Corps of Retired Executives) and ACE (Active Corps of Executives) for one-on-one counseling. SCORE is an organization of retired business executives who volunteer their services to help small business owners solve their problems; these people represent the entire range of American enterprise. The SCORE counselor's services are free, except for out-of-pocket expenses. ACE was begun to increase SCORE's Services and to keep management counseling on a continually updated basis; volunteers are active executives from all major industries, trade associations, and educational institutions.

SBA also sponsors workshops for prospective small business owners at little cost to attendees. Advice is given on tax regulations, insurance requirements, good management practices, and preparation regarding necessary capital before an individual gets into his or her own business. The counselors may suggest you delay starting a business due to certain foreseen difficulties.

For more information, write the SBA office nearest you; check your local telephone directory under United States Government.

CHECKLIST FOR STARTING YOUR BUSINESS

Before entering the filmmaking business (that is, if you are not already in the business), you should complete the following checklist. The use of this type of checklist is highly recommended by the Small Business Administration. Careful thought in advance will help you prevent mistakes and possibly avoid losing the savings of a lifetime. So many factors must be considered that unless some kind of guideline is followed conscientiously, there is danger of losing objectivity and overlooking important matters.

Obviously, this list does not cover everything; no list could. It should be used as a starter. Each point in this checklist is presented as a question designed to stimulate consideration of an important topic. Before deciding to ignore any question, you should satisfy yourself completely that it does not apply to your particular case.

Are you the type?

Have you carefully considered those qualities in which you are weak and taken steps to improve them or gotten an associate whose strong points will compensate for them? ☐

What are your chances for success?

Are general business conditions in the city and neighborhood where you are planning to locate good or bad? ☐

Are current conditions in the filmmaking business good or bad? ☐

What will be your return on investment?

How much will you have to invest in the new business? ☐

What net profit do you expect? ☐

Will the net profit divided by the investment result in a rate of return that compares favorably with the rate you can obtain from other investment opportunities? ☐

How much capital will you need?

What income can you reasonably expect in the first six months? The first year? The second year? ☐

What gross profit do you expect? ☐

What expenses can you forecast as being necessary? ☐

Is your own salary included in these expenses? ☐

Are the net profit and salary adequate? ☐

Have you compared this income with what you could make as an employee? ☐

Are you willing to risk uncertain or irregular income for the next year? Two years? ☐

Have you made an estimate of the capital you will need to open and operate this business until income equals expenses? ☐

Where can you get the money?

How much have you saved that you can put into the business immediately? ☐

How much do you have in the form of other assets which you could, if necessary, sell or on which you could borrow to get additional funds? ☐

Have you some source from which you could borrow money to put into the business? ☐

Have you talked to a banker? What does he or she think about your plan? ☐

Do you have a financial reserve available for unexpected needs? ☐

How does the total capital available from all sources compare with the estimated capital requirements? ☐

Should you share the ownership of your business with others?

Do you lack needed management skills that can be supplied satisfactorily by one or more partners? ☐

Do you need the financial assistance of one or more associates? ☐

If you do (or do not) share the business with associates, have you checked the features of each form of organization with an attorney (individual proprietorship, partnership, corporation) to determine which will fit your operation best? ☐

Where should you locate?

To help you choose a location, have you answered all of the questions about location raised in this book? ☐

What type of building will you need? ☐

How much space do you need? ☐

What provisions are you making for future expansion? ☐

What special features do you require, such as particular types of lighting, soundproofing, air conditioning, etc? ☐

What equipment do you need? ☐

After selecting a location, are you and the members of your family satisfied that the community will be a desirable place to live (and raise your children)? ☐

If the proposed location fails to meet nearly all your requirements, is there a sound reason why you should not wait and continue seeking a better location? ☐

How will you price your service?

Have you decided upon your price ranges? ☐

What will you have to charge for your films to cover your costs and obtain a profit? ☐

How does your fee compare with those charged by other filmmakers? ☐

What are the best methods of selling and promoting your films?

Have you outlined your promotional policy? ☐

Why do you expect clients will buy your films—price, quality, other? ☐

Are you going to advertise in the newspapers? Magazines? ☐

Are you going to use mail advertising? Radio advertising? Television advertising? ☐

What other management problems will you face?

Do you have the additional capital necessary to carry charge accounts? ☐

Have you planned how you will organize your work? ☐

Have you made a tentative plan to guide the distribution of your own time and effort? ☐

What records should you be prepared to keep?

Have you planned a bookkeeping system? ☐

Have you obtained any standard operating ratios for your business which you plan to use as guides? ☐

What additional records are necessary? ☐

Do you need any special forms or records? Can they be bought from stock? Must they be printed? ☐

Are you going to keep the records yourself? Hire a bookkeeper? ☐

What insurance problems will you have?

Has fire insurance been purchased? Are amounts sufficient? ☐

Is Workmen's Compensation coverage required? ☐

What other hazards present serious exposures to loss? Production insurance, et al? ☐

GLOSSARY OF FINANCIAL TERMS

Accelerated depreciation—Depreciation methods that write off the cost of an asset at a faster rate than that allowed under the straight-line method. There are three principal methods of accelerated depreciation: sum-of-years digits, double declining balance, and units of production.

Accruals—Continually recurring short-term liabilities. Examples are accrued wages, accrued taxes, and accrued interest.

Amortize—To liquidate on an installment basis; an amortized loan is one in which the principal amount of the loan is repaid in installments during the life of the loan.

Balloon payment—When a debt is not fully amortized, the final payment is larger than the preceding payments.

Bankruptcy—A legal procedure for formally liquidating a business carried out under the jurisdiction of courts of law.

Break-even analysis—An analytical technique for studying the relationship between fixed cost, variable cost, and profits. The break-even point represents that volume of sales at which total costs equal total revenues (that is, profits equal zero).

Capital asset—An asset with a life of more than one year that is not bought and sold in the ordinary course of business.

Capital budgeting—The process of planning expenditures on assets whose returns are expected to extend beyond one year.

Capital gains—Profits on the sale of capital assets held for six months or more.

Capital losses—Losses on the sale of capital assets.

Cash budget—A schedule showing cash flows (receipts, disbursements, and net cash) for a firm over a specified period.

Cash cycle—The length of time between the purchase of raw materials and the collection of accounts receivable generated in the sale of the final product.

Collateral—Assets that are used to secure a loan.

Compound interest—An interest arrangement that permits interest in succeeding periods is earned not only on the initial principal but also on the accumulated interest of prior periods. Compound interest is contrasted to simple interest in which returns are not earned on interest received.

Cost of capital—The discount rate that should be used in the capital budgeting process.

Cut-off point—In the capital budgeting process, the minimum rate of return on acceptable investment opportunities.

Debt ratio—Total debt divided by total assets.

Discount rate—The interest rate used in the discounting process; sometimes called capitalization rate.

Equity—The net worth of a business, consisting of capital stock, capital (or paid-in) surplus, earned surplus (or retained earnings), and occasionally certain net worth reserves. The terms common stock, net worth, and equity are frequently used interchangeably.

Expected return—The rate of return a firm expects to realize from an investment. The expected return is the mean value of the probability distribution of possible returns.

Expenses—The cost of assets used up or expired in order to generate revenue.

Fixed charges—Costs that do not vary with the level of output.

Income—Revenue less expenses.

Leverage factor—The ratio of debt to total assets.

Line of credit—An arrangement whereby a financial institution (bank or insurance company) commits itself to lend up to a specified maximum amount of funds during a specified period. Sometimes the interest rate on the loan is specified; at other times, it is not. Sometimes a commitment fee is imposed for obtaining the line of credit.

Liquidity—Refers to a firm's cash position and its ability to meet maturing obligations.

Margin Profit on Sales—The profit margin is the percentage of profit after tax to sales.

Marginal cost—The cost of an additional unit. The marginal cost of capital is the cost of an additional dollar of new funds.

Marginal revenue—The additional gross revenue produced by selling one additional unit of output.

Net worth—The capital and surplus of a firm (capital stock); capital surplus (paid-in capital); earned surplus (retained earnings); and, occasionally, certain reserves. For some purposes, preferred stock is included; generally, net worth refers only to the common stockholder's position.

Ordinary income—Income from the normal operations of a firm. Operating income specifically excludes income from the sale of capital assets.

Out-of-pocket costs—Costs that require current outlays of funds.

Profit margin—The ratio of profits after taxes to sales.

Retained earnings—Profits after taxes that are retained in the business rather than being paid out in dividends.

Revenue—Monetary measurement of goods and services transferred to clients.

Surtax—A tax levied in addition to the normal tax. For example, the normal corporate tax rate is 22 percent, but a surtax of 26 percent is added to the normal tax on all corporate income exceeding $25,000.

Variable costs—A cost which changes proportionately with output; often out-of-pocket and escapable, but not always.

Working capital—Refers to a firm's investment in short-term assets—cash, short-term securities, accounts receivable, and inventories. Gross working capital is defined as a firm's total current assets. Net working capital is defined as current assets minus current liabilities. If the term "working capital" is used without further qualification, it generally refers to gross working capital.

Yield—The rate of return on an investment.

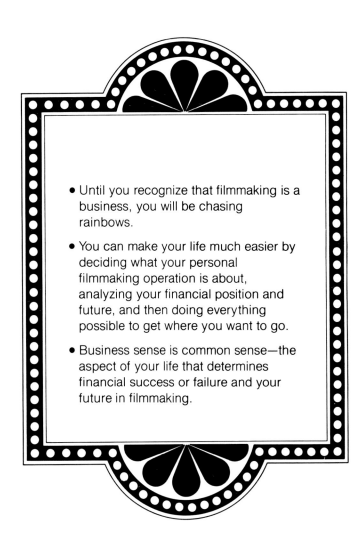

- Until you recognize that filmmaking is a business, you will be chasing rainbows.

- You can make your life much easier by deciding what your personal filmmaking operation is about, analyzing your financial position and future, and then doing everything possible to get where you want to go.

- Business sense is common sense—the aspect of your life that determines financial success or failure and your future in filmmaking.

PART SEVEN— REFERENCES

COPYRIGHT INFORMATION

The Copyright Office is, of course, the prime source of information on all questions pertaining to the copyright of films. The address of the officer in charge of publication information is Reference Division, Copyright Office, The Library of Congress, Washington, D.C. 20540. A complete list of all the pertinent circulars can be obtained by sending your request letter to the office. Three titles of particular interest are "Circular 1—General Information on Copyright," "Circular 22—How to Investigate the Copyright Status of a Work," and "Circular 91—Copyright Law of the United States of America."

As of January 1, 1978, the new Copyright Law grants protection for a film ("an original work of authorship") for the lifetime of the owner of the work plus 50 years. The current registration fee for a claim to Copyright for a motion picture is $6.00.

Copyright registration of your production does not necessarily guarantee that the film will not be transferred to videotape or some other medium. If you have secured Copyright registration with the Library of Congress and discover an unauthorized copy of your work, the fact that it was registered gives you solid ground to initiate litigation in court (unless the court rules that the transfer was not intended to deprive you of profit). At this point, you would be well advised to see a competent attorney, preferably one versed in copyright law. (Consult your local bar association or the Yellow Pages of your phone book.) Your attorney can assist you regarding disputes over copyright ownership, getting a work published, obtaining royalty payments, or prosecuting possible infringers.

TRADE UNIONS

There are so many trade unions directly associated with the filmmaking business that it is impossible to list them all in this book; for current, detailed information on any particular trade union, consult one of the following resource publications:

International Motion Picture Almanac
Quigley Publications
159 West 53rd Street
New York, New York 10019

The Motion Picture Marketplace
Little, Brown, and Company
34 Beacon Street
Boston, Massachusetts 02114

MAJOR FILM ASSOCIATIONS

American Film Institute: The American Film Institute is an independent, nonprofit organization serving the public interest: established in 1967 by the National Endowment for the Arts to advance the arts of film and television in America. The Institute preserves films, operates an advanced conservatory for filmmakers, gives assistance to new American filmmakers through grants and internships, provides guidance to film teachers and educators, publishes film books, periodicals and reference works, supports basic research, and operates a national film repertory exhibition program. The journal of the American Film Institute is American Film, published ten times a year and dedicated to the philosophy of the Institute. Yearly subscription includes membership in the Institute. Direct your correspondence to The American Film Institute, John F. Kennedy Center for the Performing Arts, Washington, D.C. 20566.

The University Film Association: The University Film Association focuses on the problems and substance in teaching the fields of film production, history, theory, criticism, and aesthetics. For membership information, write to Executive Officer, University Film Association, Dept. of Cinema Studies, New York University, New York, New York 10003.

Educational Film Library Association: The Educational Film Library Association is a national, nonprofit organization, whose primary purpose is to stimulate the use of film for educational purposes. EFLA provides: critical evaluations of newly released films, a quarterly magazine, and occasional seminars on topics of concern to members. The Association also sponsors the American Film Festival, a major nontheatrical event held annually in New York City. For membership information, write to Educational Film Library Association, 43 West 61st Street, New York, New York 10023.

FILM LABORATORY SERVICES

Your postproduction needs (from camera-original film processing to production of release prints) can be satisfied by one or more film processing labs, editing equipment rental houses, optical houses, sound recording studios, etc. For listings of professional motion picture labs, consult the *Audiovisual Marketplace, A Multimedia Guide,* 1978 Edition, R. R. Bowker Company, 1180 Avenue of Americas, New York, New York 10036, or the *Motion Picture TV and Theatre Directory,* Motion Picture Enterprises, Inc., Tarrytown, New York 10591. Each of the directories is available at your local public library.

FILM DISTRIBUTORS

When you are aiming for broad film distribution, a specialized film distributor can do much more than distribute prints, as covered in Part V. You will find a wide range of support services in these firms, from promotion to film maintenance. For a comprehensive listing of distributors, consult the *Audiovisual Marketplace, A Multimedia Guide,* 1978 Edition, R. R. Bowker Company, 1180 Avenue of Americas, New York, New York 10036.

BUSINESS FORMS

Did you ever consider having your own personalized invoice forms, purchase order forms, register forms, correspondence forms, and check-writing system? These documents are available to help you more effectively manage your filmmaking business.

Consult the Yellow Pages of your telephone directory under "Business Forms and Systems" for the suppliers nearest you. Or, check the Thomas Register at your local public library.

ADDITIONAL REFERENCES

This book deals with many business decisions that will confront the aspiring or practicing producer/filmmaker. However, you will want to dig deeper into some of the topics discussed.

An excellent source is the Small Business Administration (SBA), an agency of the federal government. The SBA offers a diverse selection of management publications, counseling services, and seminars designed to assist owner-managers or prospective owners of small businesses.

Get first-hand information at one of the SBA regional offices. Check your local telephone directory under "U.S. Government" for the office nearest you, or write the Office of Information, Small Business Administration, 1441 L Street N.W., Washington, D.C. 20416.

The local Chamber of Commerce may also maintain a business library or sponsor meetings and seminars that can help you. Your banker may be able to provide business and financial references. The Bank of America publishes a series of booklets on small business management. For a listing of current titles, write to Bank of America, Department 3120, P.O. Box 37000, San Francisco, California 94137.

You may also find the books listed below will give valuable information on many of the areas covered in this book:

Small Business Management
H. N. Broom and J. G. Longnecker
South-Western Publishing Company
Cincinnati, Ohio, 1971 Edition

Up Your Own Organization
Donald M. Dible
The Entrepreneur Press
Santa Clara, California, 1971 Edition

How to Run a Small Business
J. K. Lasser Institute
 (B. Griesman, Editor)
McGraw Hill, New York, 1974 Edition

Accounting Handbook for Nonaccountants
Clarence B. Nickerson
Cahners Publishing Company
Boston, Massachusetts, 1975 Edition

KODAK RESOURCES

MOTION PICTURE FILMS FOR THE FILMMAKER

There are a number of important requirements to consider when choosing the right film for a particular application. Briefly, they include: (1) the finished form of the motion picture—color or black-and-white, silent or sound, (2) the amount of lighting available and the film speed, (3) the amount of filtration required, if any, (4) release format— 35 mm, 16 mm, or super 8, (5) the number of release prints required, if any, (6) the type of laboratory processing and printing facilities available (reversal/ negative-positive), finally, (7) the filmmaker's personal preference.

Black-and-White Camera Films

Reversal: If economy is a factor, black-and-white reversal film should be considered. After processing, it yields positive images directly on the film exposed in the camera, and that film can be used for projection. A laboratory can produce reversal release prints from the original or produce an internegative from which multiple prints can be made.

Negative: After processing, black-and-white negative film yields negative images on the film exposed in the camera. A positive print must be made from this for evaluation, editing, and projection. Generally, negative films are used when the original is not going to be used directly or immediately, when special effects are needed, or when many release prints are required.

Color Camera Films

Reversal: After processing, color reversal films yield positive images directly on the film exposed in the camera. The film can then be used for direct projection; a most typical application for this type of film is in the television news industry. If copies of the film are needed, the same duplicating procedures apply that were discussed under Black-and-White Camera Films, Reversal. (*EASTMAN EKTACHROME* Commercial Film 7252 is a reversal camera film used to produce low-contrast originals from which excellent projection-contrast color release prints can be made; it is not recommended for direct projection.)

Negative: After processing, color negative camera film yields negative images on the film exposed in the camera. A positive print must be made for evaluation, editing, and projection. When a large number of high-quality, economical release prints are needed, color negative material should be used. The availability of laboratory processing and printing services should be thoroughly checked before you shoot your motion picture on negative stock.

Film Characteristic Summary

For your convenience, we have summarized on the next two pages the basic camera and print film characteristics (both black-and-white and color) you will need in choosing the film best suited to your needs. Detailed data sheets on each of the films listed are also available.

CAMERA FILMS

NAME OF FILM	FILM CODE NO.			TYPE	EXPOSURE INDEX		PRIMARY PURPOSE
	35 mm	16 mm	super 8		Daylight	Tungsten (3200 K)	
EASTMAN DOUBLE-X Negative Film	5222	7222	—	Black-and-White Negative	250	200	Exterior and interior photography under adverse lighting conditions
EASTMAN 4-X Negative Film	5224	7224	—	Black-and-White Negative	500	400	Newsreel work and general exterior and interior photography under adverse lighting conditions
EASTMAN PLUS-X Negative Film	5231	7231	—	Black-and-White Negative	80	64	General exterior and interior photography under average lighting conditions
EASTMAN EKTACHROME Video News Film (Daylight)	5239	7239	—	Color Reversal	160	40* (With KODAK WRATTEN Gelatin Filter No. 80A)	Very low illumination conditions or high-speed photography applications
EASTMAN EKTACHROME Video News Film (Tungsten)	5240	7240	—	Color Reversal	80* (With KODAK WRATTEN Gelatin Filter No. 85B)	125*	Color news photography. Suitable for television broadcast
KODAK EKTACHROME EF Film (Daylight)	5241	7241	—	Color Reversal	160*	40* (With KODAK WRATTEN Gelatin Filter No. 80A)	Very low illumination conditions or high-speed photography applications
KODAK EKTACHROME EF Film (Tungsten)	5242	7242	7242†	Color Reversal	80* (With KODAK WRATTEN Gelatin Filter No. 85B)	125*	Difficult lighting conditions, both exterior and interior
KODAK EKTACHROME SM Film (Type A)	—	—	7244†	Color Reversal	100 (With KODAK WRATTEN Gelatin Filter No. 85)	160	Nighttime sports events, industrial and educational photography without supplementary lighting
EASTMAN Color Negative II Film	5247	7247	—	Color Negative	64 (With KODAK WRATTEN Gelatin Filter No. 85)	100	Basic motion picture production under low lighting conditions
EASTMAN EKTACHROME Video News Film High Speed (Tungsten)	—	7250	—	Color Reversal	250* (With KODAK WRATTEN Gelatin Filter No. 85B)	400*	Color news photography under low lighting for television broadcast.
EASTMAN EKTACHROME Commercial Film	—	7252	—	Color Reversal	16 (With KODAK WRATTEN Gelatin Filter No. 85)	25	Provides low-contrast originals for color release prints of good projection contrast
KODAK EKTACHROME MS Film	5256	7256	—	Color Reversal	64	—	Low daylight illumination conditions
KODAK PLUS-X Reversal Film	—	7276	7276	Black-and-White Reversal	50	40	General exterior photography. News coverage; documentary production; kinescope recordings
KODAK 4-X Reversal Film	—	7277	7277	Black-and-White Reversal	400	320	News and sports events under limited available light
KODAK TRI-X Reversal Film	—	7278	7278	Black-and-White Reversal	200	160	Television studio photography. News and sports events under adverse artificial lighting conditions

*For the exposure index values with lighting conditions other than those given above, consult the Kodak film data sheets.

†Super 8 200-ft (61 m) cartridge also available.

RELEASE PRINT AND SPECIAL POSITIVE FILMS

NAME OF FILM	FILM CODE NO.			TYPE	EXPOSURE INDEX		PRIMARY PURPOSE
	35 mm	16 mm	super 8*		Daylight	Tungsten (3200 K)	
EASTMAN Fine Grain Release Positive Film	5302	7302	7302	Black-and-White Positive	—	—	General release printing; negative and positive titles; dubbing prints for sound
EASTMAN Direct MP Film	5360	7360	—	Black-and-White Reversal	—	—	Producing workprints and musical scoring prints for editing purposes
EASTMAN Reversal BW Print Film	—	7361	7361	Black-and-White Reversal	—	—	Use when only one or two prints are required
EASTMAN High Contrast Positive Film	5362	7362	—	Black-and-White Positive	—	—	For applications requiring high-contrast prints
EASTMAN Color Print Film	5381	7381	7381	Color Positive	—	—	General release prints Process ECP
EASTMAN Color SP Print Film	5383	7383	7383	Color Positive	—	—	General release prints Process ECP-2
EASTMAN Reversal Color Print Film	—	7387	7387	Color Reversal	—	—	General release prints
EASTMAN EKTACHROME R Print Film	5389	7389	7389	Color Reversal	—	—	Prints with same contrast as originals
EASTMAN EKTACHROME Print Film	—	7390	—	Color Reversal	—	—	General release prints
EASTMAN EKTACHROME VN Print Film	5399	7399	—	Color Reversal	—	—	Prints with same contrast as originals.

*Supplied in 35 mm and 16 mm widths perforated for super 8 format.

STANDARD ROLL LENGTHS (IN FEET)

	35 mm		16 mm	
	Color	Black-and-White	Color	Black-and-White
Camera Films*	100, 200, 400, 1000 (special order, 2000)	100, 200, 400, 1000, and in some cases, 2000	100, 200, 400, 1200	100, 200, 400, 1200
Release Print Films	1000, 2000, 3000	1000, 2000 (special order, 3000)	1200, 2000	400, 1200, 2000
Sound Recording Films	—	1000, 2000 (special order, 3000)	—	400, 1200, 2400
Television Recording Films	—	1000, 3000	—	1200, 2400
Duplicating Films	1000, 2000	1000, 2000	1000, 1200, 2000	400, 1200, 2000

*Camera films are normally supplied on spools for loading in subdued light when purchased in 100- and 200-ft rolls. Other lengths of camera films and other film types are usually supplied on cores for darkroom loading.

KODAK PUBLICATIONS

Eastman Kodak Company's Motion Picture and Audiovisual Markets Division also produces a wide selection of data books and pamphlets addressing many different filmmaking topics. Described below are some of the Kodak publications that we think will be of particular interest to those of you working or planning to work in the field of motion picture production.

Pamphlets

KODAK SONOTRACK Coating and Sound Duplicating Service (D-27)

This booklet explains how you can have *KODAK SONOTRACK* Coating applied to your silent original film or have the sound on your super 8 camera original film transferred to a *KODAK* Color Movie Film Duplicate. Some of the topics covered include: preparing the film, splicing considerations, exposing 16 mm film perforated along one edge, and cleaning and storing your film.

Movies with a Purpose (V1-13)

A communicator's guide to single-concept films. Among many of the areas covered are the use of planning cards, selecting and using a movie camera, lighting techniques, continuity, and many more helpful hints on moviemaking.

VIDEOfilm NOTES (H-40- series)

VIDEOfilm NOTES is a series of articles covering subjects such as television sound reproduction, super 8 film in television, television film editing and splicing techniques, care and handling of television film, film processing for television stations, and many more informative topics.

Motion Picture Production—The Basics of Cinematography (V1-34)

This illustrated script is intended for the camera operator, editor, and film director beginning work at the professional level. It discusses sequence development and pictorial continuity in motion picture production.

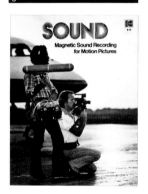

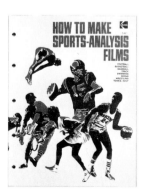

Data Books

P-18

Basic Production Techniques for Motion Pictures; 6/76; $3 This Data Book is intended to assist individuals and groups in business, education, government, industry, medicine, etc, in making effective motion picture films. It is directed primarily to the beginning producer of small-scale, in-plant motion pictures and covers planning, equipment, films, lighting, editing, titling, sound, filmmaking language, special applications, etc.

H-1

Selection and Use of *KODAK* and *EASTMAN* Motion Picture Films; 12/76; $3 This Data Book is intended to help those engaged in motion picture film production choose the film or films best suited to their particular application and obtain the best results from the stocks selected. Subjects covered include emulsion characteristics, filters, printing, processing, sound, physical characteristics, packaging, film care and storage, and industry standards. Price includes choice of current film data sheets.

S-75

SOUND: Magnetic Sound Recording for Motion Pictures; 12/77; $6.25 This Data Book illustrates the vital role played by the sound track of any motion picture, and will familiarize the reader with today's techniques in achieving top-quality sound reproduction.

S-21

Basic Titling and Animation for Motion Pictures; 12/76; $2.50 This Data Book addresses the needs of small-scale producers (such as the teacher, trainer, in-plant photographer, curriculum coordinator, and audiovisual director) concerning the production and use of titles and animated sequences in motion picture communications.

S-62

How to Make Sports-Analysis Films; 12/75; $2.65 This Data Book will acquaint the nonprofessional motion picture photographer with the basic techniques of making sports-analysis films. Subjects covered include appropriate motion picture cameras, films, projectors and filming/projection techniques for football, basketball, track and field events, swimming and diving, wrestling, golf, and tennis.

Literature Packets

For your future convenience, the publications described above, this book (H-55), and a variety of appropriate catalogs and resource listings have been gathered together as the *Basic Filmmaker's Packet,* Kodak Publication No. H-100. Taken as a whole, the packet provides many practical and up-to-date insights into the fascinating realm of professional filmmaking—information that will help you satisfy both today's *and* tomorrow's challenging communication needs. At $24.50, the H-100 packet is priced significantly lower than the total cost of all of the publications purchased separately.

Two more equally comprehensive information packets covering different areas of film application are also available. The *Basic 2 x 2-Inch Slide Packet,* Kodak Publication No. S-100 ($20.00) presents a wide range of subjects of interest to the professional slide program designer and user. And the *Film-In-Television Packet,* Kodak Publication No. H-200 ($9.00), provides broad coverage on the many uses of still and motion picture films in the television environment.

Ordering Information

A large selection of Kodak publications, including those described in this data book, are usually stocked and sold by dealers in Kodak audiovisual products (see the Yellow Pages of your telephone directory under Audio-Visual Equipment & Supplies). If your dealer cannot supply these books, you may order by title and code number from Eastman Kodak Company, Department 454, Rochester, N.Y. 14650. Please enclose your check or money order with the order, including your state and local sales taxes and $1.00 for handling. Prices shown are suggested prices only and are subject to change without notice. Actual selling prices are determined by the dealer.

For a complete listing of Kodak motion picture and audiovisual publications, tear off the reply card at the back of this book and drop it in the mail, or write to Dept. 412L (at the above address) for one free copy of *MP&AVMD Publications Index* (S-4).